Fix-It and Forget-It

PLANT-BASED COMFORT FOOD
Cookbook

127 Healthy Instant Pot & Slow Cooker Meals

HOPE COMERFORD

Good Books

New York, New York

To my good friend, Maria:

Thank you for always supporting my endeavors and for answering all my crazy cooking questions! You inspire and amaze me with your creativity in and out of the kitchen. Thank you!

Copyright © 2021 by Good Books
Photos by Bonnie Matthews and Meredith Special Interest Media

Good Books books may be purchased in bulk at special discounts for sales promotion, corporate gifts, fund-raising, or educational purposes. Special editions can also be created to specifications. For details, contact the Special Sales Department, Good Books, 307 West 36th Street, 11th Floor, New York, NY 10018 or info@skyhorsepublishing.com.

Good Books is an imprint of Skyhorse Publishing, Inc.®, a Delaware corporation.

Visit our website at www.goodbooks.com.

10 9 8 7 6 5 4 3 2

Library of Congress Cataloging-in-Publication Data
Names: Comerford, Hope, author.
Title: Fix-it and forget-it plant-based comfort food cookbook : 127 healthy slow cooker & instant pot meals / Hope Comerford.
Description: New York, New York : Good Books, [2020] | Series: Fix-it and forget-it | Includes index. | Summary: "Easy vegan recipes for your slow cooker or Instant Pot-from the New York Times bestselling series! If you're ready to include more meatless, dairy-free, egg-free, plant-based dishes in your cooking, this cookbook is for you. And if you want to cook confidently for your vegan friends or family, Fix-It and Forget-It Plant-Based Comfort Food Cookbook is full of tasty ideas. Here are slow cooker and Instant Pot breakfasts, dinners, side dishes, and desserts that you can make with confidence! All of the recipes are easy to prepare and made with easy-to-find ingredients. Here are tried and true comfort food favorites. And you'll discover lots of fresh ideas, too! Experience how enticing and satisfying plant-based cooking can be!"—Provided by publisher.
Identifiers: LCCN 2020034601 (print) | LCCN 2020034602 (ebook) | ISBN
  9781680996241 (paperback) | ISBN 9781680996814 (ebook)
Subjects: LCSH: Vegan cooking. | Vegetarian cooking. | Comfort food. |
  LCGFT: Cookbooks.
Classification: LCC TX837 .C5927 2020 (print) | LCC TX837 (ebook) | DDC
  641.5/636—dc23
LC record available at https://lccn.loc.gov/2020034601
LC ebook record available at https://lccn.loc.gov/2020034602

Cover design by Mona Lin
Cover photo by Meredith Special Interest Media

Print ISBN: 978-1-68099-624-1
Ebook ISBN: 978-1-68099-681-4

Printed in China

Contents

Welcome to *Fix-It and Forget-It Plant-Based Comfort Food Cookbook*

What is a plant-based diet? Well, a plant-based diet is one that involves eating whole, real foods that come from plants. This includes fruits and vegetables, nuts, seeds, oils, whole grains, legumes, and beans. How is plant-based different than a vegan diet? That's a great question! Vegans do not consume or wear animal products, but those following a plant-based diet just try to avoid animal and dairy products. Overall, they are very similar diets.

This book contains 127 plant-based comfort food recipes you will love! We've got you covered from breakfast to dessert . . . all made in your slow cooker or Instant Pot. You'll love recipes like Apple Cinnamon Oatmeal, Tofu Lettuce Wraps, Minestrone, Chickpea Tortilla Soup, Swedish Cabbage Rolls, Spicy Orange Tofu, German Potato Salad, and Pineapple Bread Pudding! Is your mouth watering yet? It will be, as you flip from delicious recipe to delicious recipe!

As you begin journeying through this book, I always suggest reading from cover to cover. I can't tell you the good recipes I've passed on in the past by not following this advice. Don't become overwhelmed. Bookmark, or dog-ear the pages of the recipes that interest you the most as you go through. Then, when you've looked at everything, go back to those marked pages and pick 2–3 to start with. You may even consider choosing a recipe or two you already have the ingredients on hand for. If not, start that grocery list and get to your local store and grab only what you need.

Any specialized diet can be tricky if you're not used to it yet, which is why we've taken the guesswork out for you. If you're already a seasoned plant-based consumer, we can't wait for you to fall in love with the recipes in this book to add to the collection you already have. Enjoy discovering the incredible recipes in *Fix-It and Forget-It Plant-Based Comfort Food*!

Choosing a Slow Cooker

Not all slow cookers are created equal . . . or work equally as well for everyone!

Those of us who use slow cookers frequently know we have our own preferences when it comes to which slow cooker we choose to use. For instance, I love my programmable slow cooker, but there are many programmable slow cookers I've tried that I've strongly disliked. Why? Because some go by increments of 15 or 30 minutes and some go by 4, 6, 8, or 10 hours. I dislike those restrictions, but I have family and friends who don't mind them at all! I am also pretty brand loyal when it comes to my manual slow cookers because I've had great success with those and have had unsuccessful moments with slow cookers of other brands. So, which slow cooker(s) is/are best for your household?

It really depends on how many people you're feeding and if you're gone for long periods of time. Here are my recommendations:

For 2–3 person household	3–5 quart slow cooker
For 4–5 person household	5–6 quart slow cooker
For a 6+ person household	6½–7 quart slow cooker

Large slow cooker advantages/disadvantages:

Advantages:
- You can fit a loaf pan or a baking dish into a 6- or 7-quart, depending on the shape of your cooker. That allows you to make bread or cakes, or even smaller quantities of main dishes. (Take your favorite baking dish and loaf pan along when you shop for a cooker to make sure they'll fit inside.)
- You can feed large groups of people, or make larger quantities of food, allowing for leftovers, or meals, to freeze.

Disadvantages:
- They take up more storage room.
- They don't fit as neatly into a dishwasher.
- If your crock isn't ⅔–¾ full, you may burn your food.

Small slow cooker advantages/disadvantages:

Advantages:
- They're great for lots of appetizers, for serving hot drinks, for baking cakes straight in the crock, and for dorm rooms or apartments.
- Great option for making recipes of smaller quantities.

Disadvantages:
- Food in smaller quantities tends to cook more quickly than larger amounts. So keep an eye on it.
- Chances are, you won't have many leftovers. So, if you like to have leftovers, a smaller slow cooker may not be a good option for you.

My recommendation:

Have at least two slow cookers; one around 3 to 4 quarts and one 6 quarts or larger. A third would be a huge bonus (and a great advantage to your cooking repertoire!). The advantage of having at least a couple is you can make a larger variety of recipes. Also, you can make at least two or three dishes at once for a whole meal.

Manual vs. Programmable

If you are gone for only six to eight hours a day, a manual slow cooker might be just fine for you. If you are gone for more than eight hours during the day, I would highly recommend purchasing a programmable slow cooker that will switch to warm when the cook time you set is up. It will allow you to cook a wider variety of recipes.

The two I use most frequently are my 4-quart manual slow cooker and my 6½-quart programmable slow cooker. I like that I can make smaller portions in my 4-quart slow cooker on days I don't need or want leftovers, but I also love how my 6½-quart slow cooker can accommodate whole chickens, turkey breasts, hams, or big batches of soups. I use them both often.

Get to know your slow cooker . . .

Plan a little time to get acquainted with your slow cooker. Each slow cooker has its own personality—just like your oven (and your car). Plus, many new slow cookers cook hotter and faster than earlier models. I think that with all of the concern for food safety, the slow cooker manufacturers have amped up their settings so that "High," "Low," and "Warm" are all higher temperatures than in the older models. That means they cook hotter—and therefore, faster—than the first slow cookers. The beauty of these little machines is that they're supposed to cook low and slow. We count on that when we flip the switch in the morning before we leave the house for ten hours or so. So, because none of us knows what kind of temperament our slow cooker has until we try it out, nor how hot it cooks—don't assume anything. Save yourself a disappointment and make the first recipe in your new slow cooker on a day when you're at home. Cook it for the shortest amount of time the recipe calls for. Then, check the food to see if it's done. Or if you start smelling food that seems to be finished, turn off the cooker and rescue your food.

Also, all slow cookers seem to have a "hot spot," which is of great importance to know, especially when baking with your slow cooker. This spot may tend to burn food in that area if you're not careful. If you're baking directly in your slow cooker, I recommend covering the "hot spot" with some foil.

Take notes . . .

Don't be afraid to make notes in your cookbook. It's yours! Chances are, it will eventually get passed down to someone in your family and they will love and appreciate all of your musings. Take note of which slow cooker you used and exactly how long it took to cook the recipe. The next time you make it, you won't need to try to remember. Apply what you learned to the next recipes you make in your cooker. If another recipe says it needs to cook 7–9 hours, and you've discovered your slow cooker cooks on the faster side, cook that recipe for 6–6½ hours and then check it. You can always cook a recipe longer—but you can't reverse things if it's overdone.

Get creative . . .

If you know your morning is going to be hectic, prepare everything the night before, take it out so the crock warms up to room temperature when you first get up in the morning, then plug it in and turn it on as you're leaving the house.

If you want to make something that has a short cook time and you're going to be gone longer than that, cook it the night before and refrigerate it for the next day. Warm it up when you get home. Or, cook those recipes on the weekend when you know you'll be home and eat them later in the week.

Slow Cooking Tips and Tricks and Other Things You May Not Know

- Slow cookers tend to work best when they're ⅔ to ¾ of the way full. You may need to increase the cooking time if you've exceeded that amount, or reduce it if you've put in less than that. If you're going to exceed that limit, it would be best to reduce the recipe, or split it between two slow cookers. (Remember how I suggested owning at least two or three slow cookers?)
- Keep the lid on! Every time you take a peek, you lose 20 minutes of cooking time. Please take this into consideration each time you lift the lid! I know, some of you can't help yourself and are going to lift anyway. Just don't forget to tack on 20 minutes to your cook time for each time you peeked!
- Sometimes it's beneficial to remove the lid. If you'd like your dish to thicken a bit, take the lid off during the last half hour to hour of cooking time.
- If you have a big slow cooker (7- to 8-quart), you can cook a small batch in it by putting the recipe ingredients into an oven-safe baking dish or baking pan and then placing that into the cooker's crock. First, put a trivet or some metal jar rings on the bottom of the crock, and then set your dish or pan on top of them. Or a loaf pan may "hook onto" the top ridges of the crock belonging to a large oval cooker and hang there straight and securely, "baking" a cake or quick bread. Cover the cooker and flip it on.
- The outside of your slow cooker will be hot! Please remember to keep it out of reach of children and keep that in mind for yourself as well!
- Add fresh herbs 10 minutes before the end of the cooking time to maximize their flavor.
- If your recipe calls for cooked pasta, add it 10 minutes before the end of the cooking time if the cooker is on High; 30 minutes before the end of the cooking time if it's on Low. Then the pasta won't get mushy.
- Cooked beans freeze well. Store them in freezer bags (squeeze the air out first) or freezer boxes. Cooked and dried bean measurements:
    - 16-oz. can, drained = about 1¾ cups beans
    - 19-oz. can, drained = about 2 cups beans
    - 1 lb. dried beans (about 2½ cups) = 5 cups cooked beans

What Is an Instant Pot?

In short, an Instant Pot is a digital pressure cooker that also has multiple other functions. Not only can it be used as a pressure cooker, but depending on which model Instant Pot you have, you can set it to do things like sauté, cook rice, multigrains, porridge, soup/stew, beans/chili, porridge, meat, poultry, cake, eggs, yogurt, steam, slow cook, or even set it manually. Because the Instant Pot has so many functions, it takes away the need for multiple appliances on your counter and uses fewer pots and pans.

Getting Started with Your Instant Pot

Get to Know Your Instant Pot . . .

The very first thing most Instant Pot owners do is called the water test. It helps you get to know your Instant Pot a bit, familiarizes you with it, and might even take a bit of your apprehension away (because if you're anything like me, I was scared to death to use it!).

Step 1: Plug in your Instant Pot. This may seem obvious to some, but when we're nervous about using a new appliance, sometimes we forget things like this.

Step 2: Make sure the inner pot is inserted in the cooker. You should NEVER attempt to cook anything in your device without the inner pot, or you will ruin your Instant Pot. Food should never come into contact with the actual housing unit.

Step 3: The inner pot has lines for each cup (how convenient, right?!). Fill the inner pot with water until it reaches the 3-cup line.

Step 4: Check the sealing ring to be sure it's secure and in place. You should not be able to move it around. If it's not in place properly, you may experience issues with the pot letting out a lot of steam while cooking, or not coming to pressure.

Step 5: Seal the lid. There is an arrow on the lid between and "open" and "close." There is also an arrow on the top of the base of the Instant Pot between a picture of a locked lock and an unlocked lock. Line those arrows up, then turn the lid toward the picture of the lock (left). You will hear a noise that will indicate the lid is locked. If you do not hear a noise, it's not locked. Try it again.

Step 6: ALWAYS check to see if the steam valve on top of the lid is turned to "sealing." If it's not on "sealing" and is on "venting," it will not be able to come to pressure.

Step 7: Press the "Steam" button and use the +/- arrow to set it to 2 minutes. Once it's at the desired time, you don't need to press anything else. In a few seconds, the Instant Pot will begin all on its own. For those of us with digital slow cookers, we have a tendency to look for the "start" button, but there isn't one on the Instant Pot.

Step 8: Now you wait for the "magic" to happen! The "cooking" will begin once the device comes to pressure. This can take anywhere from 5–30 minutes I've found in my experience.

Then, you will see the countdown happen (from the time you set it at). After that, the Instant Pot will beep, which means your meal is done!

Step 9: Your Instant Pot will now automatically switch to "warm" and begin a count of how many minutes it's been on warm. The next part is where you either wait for the NPR, or natural pressure release (meaning the pressure releases all on its own), or you do what's called a QR, or quick release (meaning, you manually release the pressure). Which method you choose depends on what you're cooking, but in this case, you can choose either since it's just water. For NPR, you will wait for the lever to move all the way back over to "venting" and watch the pinion (float valve) next to the lever. It will be flush with the lid when at full pressure and will drop when the pressure is done releasing. If you choose QR, be very careful not to have your hands over the vent as the steam is very hot and you can burn yourself.

The Three Most Important Buttons You Need To Know About . . .

You will find the majority of recipes will use the following three buttons:

Manual/Pressure Cook: Some older models tend to say "Manual" and the newer models seem to say "Pressure Cook." They mean the same thing. From here, you use the +/- button to change the cook time. After several seconds, the Instant Pot will begin its process. The exact name of this button will vary on your model of Instant Pot.

Sauté: Many recipes will have you sauté vegetables before beginning the pressure cooking process. For this setting, you will not use the lid of the Instant Pot.

Keep Warm/Cancel: This may just be the most important button on the Instant Pot. When you forget to use the +/- buttons to change the time for a recipe, or you press a wrong button, you can hit "keep warm/cancel" and it will turn your Instant Pot off for you.

What Do All the Buttons Do . . .

With so many buttons, it's hard to remember what each one does or means. You can use this as a quick guide in a pinch.

Soup/Broth: This button cooks at high pressure for 30 minutes. It can be adjusted using the +/- buttons to cook more for 40 minutes, or less for 20 minutes.

Meat/Stew: This button cooks at high pressure for 35 minutes. It can be adjusted using the +/- buttons to cook more for 45 minutes, or less for 20 minutes.

Bean/Chili: This button cooks at high pressure for 30 minutes. It can be adjusted using the +/- buttons to cook more for 40 minutes, or less for 25 minutes.

Poultry: This button cooks at high pressure for 15 minutes. It can be adjusted using the +/- buttons to cook more 30 minutes, or less for 5 minutes.

Rice: This button cooks at low pressure and is the only fully automatic program. It is for cooking white rice and will automatically adjust the cooking time depending on the amount of water and rice in the cooking pot.

Multigrain: This button cooks at high pressure for 40 minutes. It can be adjusted using the +/- buttons to cook more for 45 minutes of warm water soaking time and 60 minutes pressure-cooking time, or less for 20 minutes.

Porridge: This button cooks at high pressure for 20 minutes. It can be adjusted using the +/- buttons to cook more for 30 minutes, or less for 15 minutes.

Steam: This button cooks at high pressure for 10 minutes. It can be adjusted using the +/- buttons to cook more for 15 minutes, or less for 3 minutes. Always use a rack or steamer basket with this function because it heats at full power continuously while it's coming to pressure and you do not want food in direct contact with the bottom of the pressure cooking pot or it will burn. Once it reaches pressure, the steam button regulates pressure by cycling on and off, similar to the other pressure buttons.

Less | Normal | More: Adjust between the *Less | Normal | More* settings by pressing the same cooking function button repeatedly until you get to the desired setting. (Older versions use the *Adjust* button.)

+/- Buttons: Adjust the cook time up [+] or down [-]. (On newer models, you can also press and hold [-] or [+] for 3 seconds to turn sound OFF or ON.)

Cake: This button cooks at high pressure for 30 minutes. It can be adjusted using the +/- buttons to cook more for 40 minutes, or less for 25 minutes.

Egg: This button cooks at high pressure for 5 minutes. It can be adjusted using the +/- buttons to cook more for 6 minutes, or less for 4 minutes.

Instant Pot Tips and Tricks and Other Things You May Not Know

- Never attempt to cook directly in the Instant Pot without the inner pot!
- Once you set the time, you can walk away. It will show the time you set it to, then will change to the word "on" while the pressure builds. Once the Instant Pot has come to pressure, you will once again see the time you set it for. It will count down from there.

- Always make sure your sealing ring is securely in place. Many people find it useful to have a sealing ring for sweet dishes and one for savory dishes. If it shows signs of wear or tear, it needs to be replaced.
- Have a sealing ring for savory recipes and a separate sealing ring for sweet recipes. Many people report of their desserts tasting like a roast (or another savory food) if they try to use the same sealing ring for all recipes.
- The stainless steel rack (trivet) your Instant Pot comes with can used to keep food from being completely submerged in liquid, like baked potatoes or ground beef. It can also be used to set another pot on, for pot-in-pot cooking.
- If you use warm or hot liquid instead of cold liquid, you may need to adjust the cooking time, or your food may not come out done.
- Always double check to see that the valve on the lid is set to "sealing" and not "venting" when you first lock the lid. This will save you from your Instant Pot not coming to pressure.
- Use Natural Pressure Release for tougher cuts of meat, recipes with high starch (like rice or grains), and recipes with a high volume of liquid. This means you let the Instant Pot naturally release pressure. The little bobbin will fall once pressure is released completely.
- Use Quick Release for more delicate cuts of meat and vegetables–like seafood, chicken breasts, and steaming vegetables. This means you manually turn the vent (being careful not to put your hand over the vent!!!) to release the pressure. The little bobbin will fall once pressure is released completely.
- Make sure there is a clear pathway for the steam to release. The last thing you want is to ruin the bottom of your cupboards with all that steam.
- You MUST use liquid in your Instant Pot. The MINIMUM amount of liquid you should have in your inner pot is ½ cup; however, most recipe work best with at least 1 cup.
- Do NOT overfill your Instant Pot! It should only be ½ full for rice or beans (food that expands greatly when cooked), or ⅔ of the way full for most everything else. Do not fill it to the max filled line.
- In this book, the Cooking Time DOES NOT take into account the amount of time it will take your Instant Pot to come to pressure, or the amount of time it will take the Instant Pot to release pressure. Be aware of this when choosing a recipe to make.
- If your Instant Pot is not coming to pressure, it's usually because the sealing ring is not on properly, or the vent is not set to "sealing."
- The more liquid, or the colder the ingredients, the longer it will take for the Instant Pot to come to pressure.

- Always make sure that the Instant Pot is dry before inserting the inner pot, and make sure the inner pot is dry before inserting it into the Instant Pot.
- Doubling a recipe does not change the cook time, but instead it will take longer to come up to pressure.
- You do not always need to double the liquid when doubling a recipe. Depending on what you're making, more liquid may make your food too watery. Use your best judgment.
- When using the slow cooker function, use the following chart:

Slow Cooker	Instant Pot
Warm	Less or Low
Low	Normal or Medium
High	More or High

Breakfast

Granola

Hope Comerford
Clinton Township, MI

Makes about 10 cups
Prep. Time: 20 minutes ⚬ *Cooking Time: 4–6 hours* ⚬ *Ideal slow-cooker size: 6- to 7-qt.*

6 cups old-fashioned oats

¾ cup chopped almonds

½ cup chopped pecans

¾ cup raw sunflower seeds

¼ cup flaxseed

1 cup dried cranberries

1 cup chopped dehydrated apples

1 cup vegan apple butter (see recipe on pg. 37)

¼ cup vegan "honey"

¼ cup maple syrup

1. Place all of the dry ingredients in a bowl and stir.

2. Mix together the apple butter, vegan "honey," and maple syrup.

3. Spray your crock with a vegan nonstick spray.

4. Pour your granola mixture in the crock with the apple butter mixture on top. Mix thoroughly.

5. Cover and cook on Low with the lid vented for 4–6 hours, stirring frequently (every 30–40 minutes) or until the granola is lightly browned and slightly clumpy.

Apple Granola

Phyllis Good
Lancaster, PA

Makes 12 servings
Prep. Time: 20 minutes   ⚜   *Cooking Time: 2–3 hours*   ⚜   *Chilling time: 1 hour*   ⚜   *Ideal slow-cooker size: 5-qt.*

9 cups unpeeled, sliced apples
1 ½ tsp. cinnamon
1 ½ cups dry rolled oats
1 ½ cups wheat germ
1 ½ cups whole wheat flour
1 ½ cups sunflower seeds
1 ⅓ cups water
¾ cup vegan "honey"

1. Grease interior of slow cooker crock.

2. Use your food processor to slice the apples. Place slices in slow cooker.

3. Sprinkle apple slices with cinnamon, and then stir together gently.

4. In a good-sized bowl, stir together dry oats, wheat germ, whole wheat flour, and sunflower seeds.

5. When dry ingredients are well mixed, pour in water and vegan "honey." Using a sturdy spoon or your clean hands, mix thoroughly until ingredients are damp throughout.

6. Spoon over apples.

7. Cover, but vent the lid by propping it open with a chopstick or wooden spoon handle. Or if you're using an oval cooker, turn the lid sideways.

8. Cook on High for 1 hour, stirring up from the bottom and around the sides every 20 minutes or so. (Set a timer so you don't forget!)

9. Switch the cooker to Low. Bake another 1–2 hours, still stirring every 20 minutes or so.

10. Granola is done when it eventually browns a bit and looks dry.

11. Pour granola onto parchment or a large baking sheet to cool and crisp up more.

12. If you like clumps, no need to stir granola further while it cools. Otherwise, break up the granola with a spoon or your hands as it cools.

13. When completely cooled, store in airtight container.

Soy-Flax Granola

Phyllis Good
Lancaster, PA

Makes 15 servings
Prep. Time: 20 minutes ✤ Cooking Time: 1½–2½ hours
Chilling Time: 2 hours ✤ Ideal slow-cooker size: 6-qt.

12 oz. soybeans, roasted with no salt

4 cups gluten-free rolled oats

¾ cup soy flour

¾ cup ground flaxseeds

1 tsp. salt

2 tsp. cinnamon

⅔ cup coarsely chopped walnuts

⅔ cup whole pecans

¾ cup maple syrup

½ cup coconut oil, melted

¾ cup applesauce

2 tsp. vanilla extract

Optional additions: dried cranberries, dried cherries, chopped dried apricots, chopped dried figs, raisins, or some combination of these dried fruits

1. Grease interior of slow cooker crock.

2. Briefly process soybeans in a blender or food processor until coarsely chopped. Place in large bowl.

3. Add oats, flour, flaxseeds, salt, cinnamon, walnuts, and pecans. Mix thoroughly with spoon.

4. In a smaller bowl, combine maple syrup, coconut oil, applesauce, and vanilla well.

5. Pour wet ingredients over dry. Stir well, remembering to stir up from the bottom, using either a strong spoon or your clean hands.

6. Pour mixture into crock. Cover, but vent the lid by propping it open with a chopstick or wooden spoon handle. Or if you're using an oval cooker, turn the lid sideways.

7. Cook on High for 1 hour, stirring up from the bottom and around the sides every 20 minutes or so. (Set a timer so you don't forget!)

8. Switch the cooker to Low. Bake another 1–2 hours, still stirring every 20 minutes.

9. Granola is done when it eventually browns a bit and looks dry.

10. Pour granola onto parchment or a large baking sheet to cool and crisp up more.

11. Stir in any of the dried fruits that you want.

12. If you like clumps, no need to stir granola again while it cools. Otherwise, break up the granola with a spoon or your hands as it cools.

13. When completely cooled, store in airtight container.

Grain and Fruit Cereal

Cynthia Haller
New Holland, PA

Makes 4–5 servings
Prep. Time: 5 minutes ⚬ Cooking Time: 3½ hours ⚬ Ideal slow-cooker size: 4-qt.

⅓ cup uncooked quinoa
⅓ cup uncooked millet
⅓ cup uncooked brown rice
4 cups water
¼ tsp. salt
½ cup raisins or dried cranberries
¼ cup chopped nuts, optional
I tsp. vanilla extract, optional
½ tsp. ground cinnamon, optional
I Tbsp. maple syrup, optional

1. Wash the quinoa, millet, and brown rice and rinse well.

2. Place the grains, water, and salt in a slow cooker. Cook on Low until most of the water has been absorbed, about 3 hours.

3. Add dried fruit and any optional ingredients, and cook for 30 minutes more. If the mixture is too thick, add a little more water.

4. Serve hot or cold.

Serving suggestion:

Add a little non-dairy milk of your choice to each bowl of cereal before serving.

Oatmeal Morning

Barbara Forrester Landis
Lititz, PA

Makes 6 servings
Prep. Time: 10 minutes   ✤   *Cooking Time: 2½–6 hours*   ✤   *Ideal slow-cooker size: 3-qt.*

1 cup uncooked steel-cut oats
1 cup dried cranberries
1 cup walnuts
½ tsp. kosher salt
1 Tbsp. cinnamon
2 cups water
2 cups fat-free non-dairy milk (almond, rice, etc.)

1. Combine all dry ingredients in slow cooker. Stir well.

2. Add water and non-dairy milk and stir.

3. Cover. Cook on High 2½ hours, or on Low 5–6 hours.

Apple Oatmeal

Frances B. Musser
Newmanstown, PA

Makes 5 servings
Prep. Time: 20 minutes ♣ Cooking Time: 3–5 hours ♣ Ideal slow-cooker size: 3-qt.

2 cups non-dairy milk
1 cup water
1 Tbsp. vegan "honey"
1 Tbsp. coconut oil
¼ tsp. kosher salt
½ tsp. cinnamon
1 cup gluten-free steel-cut oats
1 cup chopped apples
½ cup chopped walnuts
1 Tbsp. turbinado sugar

1. Grease the inside of the slow cooker crock.

2. Add all ingredients to crock and mix.

3. Cover. Cook on Low 3–5 hours.

Apple Cinnamon Oatmeal

Hope Comerford
Clinton Township, MI

Makes 2–3 servings
Prep. Time: 5 minutes ⚘ *Cooking Time: 7 hours* ⚘ *Ideal slow-cooker size: 2-qt.*

½ cup steel-cut oats

2 cups unsweetened vanilla almond milk

1 small apple, peeled and diced

¼ tsp. cinnamon

1. Spray crock with nonstick spray.

2. Place all ingredients into crock and stir lightly.

3. Cover and cook on Low for 7 hours.

Serving suggestion:

Add a bit of sweetener of your choice if you wish at time of serving.

German Chocolate Oatmeal

Hope Comerford
Clinton Township, MI

Makes 4 servings
Prep. Time: 5 minutes ⚭ *Cooking Time: 6–8 hours* ⚭ *Ideal slow-cooker size: 3-qt.*

2 cups steel-cut oats
8 cups unsweetened coconut milk
¼ cup unsweetened cocoa powder
¼ tsp. kosher salt
sweetened shredded coconut, to taste

1. Spray crock with nonstick spray.

2. Place steel-cut oats, coconut milk, cocoa powder, and salt into crock and stir to mix.

3. Cover and cook on Low for 6–8 hours.

4. To serve, top each bowl of oatmeal with desired amount of shredded coconut.

Serving suggestion:

Sweeten with a bit of sweetener of your choice if you wish at time of serving.

Apple Breakfast Cobbler

Anona M. Teel
Bangor, PA

Makes 8 servings
Prep. Time: 25 minutes ♣ Cooking Time: 2–9 hours ♣ Ideal slow-cooker size: 4- or 5-qt.

8 medium apples, cored, peeled, sliced

2 Tbsp. maple syrup

dash of cinnamon

juice of 1 lemon

2 Tbsp. coconut oil, melted

2 cups granola (see recipe on pg. 13)

1. Combine ingredients in slow cooker.

2. Cover. Cook on Low 7–9 hours (while you sleep!), or on High 2–3 hours (after you're up in the morning).

Best Steel-Cut Oats

Colleen Heatwole
Burton, MI

Makes 4 servings
Prep. Time: 5 minutes & Cooking Time: 3 minutes
Setting: Manual & Pressure: High & Release: Natural

1 cup steel-cut oats
2 cups water
1 cup almond milk
pinch salt
½ tsp. vanilla extract
1 cinnamon stick
¼ cup raisins
¼ cup dried cherries
1 tsp. ground cinnamon
¼ cup toasted almonds
sweetener of choice, optional

1. Add all ingredients to the inner pot of the Instant Pot except the toasted almonds and sweetener.

2. Secure the lid and make sure the vent is turned to sealing. Cook 3 minutes on high, using manual function.

3. Let the pressure release naturally.

4. Remove cinnamon stick.

5. Add almonds, and sweetener if desired, and serve.

Fruit Breakfast Cobbler

Hope Comerford
Clinton Township, MI

Makes 4 servings
Prep. Time: 10 minutes ⚯ *Cooking Time: 15–20 minutes*
Setting: Steam and Sauté ⚯ *Release: Manual*

2 pears, chopped

2 sweet apples, chopped

2 peaches, diced

2 Tbsp. maple syrup

3 Tbsp. coconut oil

1 tsp. ground cinnamon

½ cup unsweetened shredded coconut

½ cup pecans, diced

2 Tbsp. flaxseed

¼ cup oats

1. Place the pears, apples, and peaches in the inner pot of your Instant Pot, then top with the maple syrup, coconut oil, and cinnamon. Lock lid and set vent to sealing.

2. Press Steam and set to 8 minutes.

3. When cook time is up, do a quick release. When lid is able to be removed, remove the fruit with a slotted spoon and place in a bowl. You want to leave the juices in the inner pot.

4. Set the Instant Pot to Sauté and put in the shredded coconut, pecan pieces, flaxseed, and oats. Stir them constantly, until the shredded coconut is lightly toasted.

5. Spoon the shredded coconut/oat mixture over the steamed fruit and enjoy.

Fiesta Hash Browns

Dena Mell-Dorchy
Royal Oak, MI

Makes 8 servings
Prep. Time: 5 minutes ♣ *Cooking Time: 6 hours* ♣ *Ideal slow-cooker size: 3- or 4-qt.*

16 oz. vegan sausage crumbles
½ cup chopped onion
5 cups vegan frozen diced hash browns
8 oz. low-sodium vegetable stock
1 small red sweet pepper
1 jalapeño, seeded and finely diced
1½ cups sliced mushrooms
2 Tbsp. quick-cooking tapioca
½ cup nutritional yeast flakes

1. Spray slow cooker with vegan nonstick spray.

2. Combine all ingredients in the crock and stir.

3. Cover and cook on Low heat for 6 hours. Stir before serving. Top with nutritional yeast flakes.

Instant Pot Applesauce

Hope Comerford
Clinton Township, MI

Makes 6 cups
Prep. Time: 10 minutes ⚬ Cooking Time: 5 minutes
Setting: Manual ⚬ Pressure: High ⚬ Release: Natural

5 lb. apples (whatever kind(s) you like),
peeled, cored, and sliced

¼ cup water

2 tsp. vanilla extract

3–4 Tbsp. lemon juice

3 Tbsp. brown sugar

¼ cup or less of white sugar

¼ tsp. cinnamon

1. Place all of the ingredients into the inner pot of the Instant Pot and give a stir.

2. Secure the lid, making sure it locks, and turn the vent to sealing.

3. Press the Manual button and set it for 5 minutes on high pressure.

4. When cooking time is up, let the pressure release naturally.

5. When pressure is done releasing, open lid, then use a potato smasher or immersion blender to make the applesauce as smooth or lumpy as you like.

TIP
You can leave the sugar out or adjust the amount for your family's needs.

Apple Butter

Hope Comerford
Clinton Township, MI

Makes 6 cups
Prep. Time: 15 minutes ❧ Cooking Time: 60 minutes ❧ Setting: Manual
Pressure: High ❧ Release: Natural

5 lb. apples, peeled, cored, and sliced
½ cup brown sugar
¼ tsp. ground cloves
½ tsp. ground nutmeg
1 Tbsp. cinnamon
pinch salt
2 Tbsp. lemon juice
1 Tbsp. vanilla extract
¼ cup water

1. Combine all of the ingredients in the inner pot of the Instant Pot and mix well.

2. Lock the lid in place; turn the vent to sealing.

3. Press Manual and set to 60 minutes on high pressure.

4. When cooking time is over, let the steam release naturally.

5. Using an immersion blender, blend the apples until smooth.

TIP
This should keep in the refrigerator for up to 3 weeks in a tightly sealed container.

Vegan Sausage and Sweet Pepper Hash

Hope Comerford
Clinton Township, MI

Makes 6–8 servings
Prep. Time: 10 minutes ⚮ Cooking Time: 6 hours ⚮ Ideal slow-cooker size: 4-qt.

14-oz. pkg. vegan Italian sausage, cut lengthwise, then into ½-inch pieces

16 oz. vegan frozen diced potatoes

1½ cups sliced sweet onion

1 yellow pepper, sliced

1 green pepper, sliced

1 red pepper, sliced

¼ cup melted vegan butter

1 tsp. sea salt

½ tsp. pepper

½ tsp. dried thyme

½ tsp. dried parsley

½ cup nutritional yeast

1. Spray crock with vegan nonstick spray.

2. Place sausage, frozen potatoes, onion, and sliced peppers into crock.

3. Mix melted vegan butter with salt, pepper, thyme, parsley, and nutritional yeast. Pour over contents of crock and stir.

4. Cover and cook on Low for 6 hours.

Appetizers & Snacks

Tofu Lettuce Wraps

Hope Comerford
Clinton Township, MI

Makes about 12 wraps
Prep. Time: 15 minutes ⚜ *Cooking Time: 2–3 hours* ⚜ *Ideal slow-cooker size: 5- or 7-qt.*

32 oz. meatless crumbles

4 cloves garlic, minced

½ cup minced sweet yellow onion

4 Tbsp. liquid aminos

1 Tbsp. natural crunchy peanut butter

1 tsp. rice wine vinegar

1 tsp. sesame oil

¼ tsp. kosher salt

¼ tsp. red pepper flakes

¼ tsp. black pepper

8-oz. can sliced water chestnuts, drained, rinsed, chopped

3 green onions, sliced

12 good-sized pieces of iceberg lettuce, rinsed and patted dry

1. In the crock, combine the meatless crumbles, garlic, yellow onion, liquid aminos, peanut butter, vinegar, sesame oil, salt, red pepper flakes, and black pepper.

2. Cover and cook on Low for 2–3 hours.

3. Add in the water chestnuts and green onions. Cover and cook for an additional 10–15 minutes.

4. Serve a good spoonful on each piece of iceberg lettuce.

Serving suggestion:

Garnish with diced red bell pepper and diced green onion.

Tomato-Zucchini Ratatouille

Barb Yoder
Angola, IN

Makes about 3½ cups, or 13 servings
Prep. Time: 20–30 minutes ⚜ *Cooking Time: 7–8 hours* ⚜ *Ideal slow-cooker size: 4-qt.*

1½ cups chopped onion

6-oz. can tomato paste

1 Tbsp. olive oil

2 cloves garlic, minced (1 tsp.)

1½ tsp. crushed dried basil

½ tsp. dried thyme

15-oz. can chopped low-sodium tomatoes, with juice drained but reserved

1 large zucchini, halved lengthwise and sliced thin

salt and pepper, to taste, optional

26 slices vegan French bread or baguette

1. Mix all ingredients except bread in slow cooker.

2. Cover. Cook on Low 7–8 hours.

3. If mixture is stiffer than you wish, stir in some reserved tomato juice.

4. Serve hot or cold on top of vegan French bread or baguette slices.

Garlicky Hoisin Mushrooms

Hope Comerford
Clinton Township, MI

Makes 10 servings
Prep. Time: 10 minutes & Cooking Time: 5–6 hours & Ideal slow-cooker size: 3-qt.

24 oz. whole button mushrooms, trimmed

1 small sweet onion, halved, sliced

¼ cup of water

3 cloves garlic, minced

2 Tbsp. liquid aminos

1 Tbsp. smooth natural peanut butter

1 tsp. rice wine vinegar

1 tsp. sesame oil

¼ tsp. crushed red pepper

1. Spray crock with nonstick spray.

2. Place mushrooms and onions into the crock.

3. In a bowl, mix together the water, garlic, liquid aminos, peanut butter, rice wine vinegar, sesame oil, and crushed red pepper. Pour this mixture over the mushrooms and onions.

4. Cover and cook on Low for 5–6 hours.

5. To serve, stir the mushrooms gently through the sauce, then remove with a slotted spoon. Serve the mushrooms with toothpicks.

Serving suggestion:

Garnish with diced green onion and sesame seeds.

Slow-Cooked Salsa

Andy Wagner
Quarryville, PA

Makes 2 cups

Prep. Time: 15 minutes ❧ Cooking Time: 2½–3 hours ❧ Standing Time: 2 hours ❧ Ideal slow-cooker size: 3-qt.

10 plum tomatoes
2 cloves garlic
1 small onion, cut into wedges
1–2 jalapeño peppers
½ cup chopped fresh cilantro
½ tsp. sea salt, optional

1. Core tomatoes. Cut a small slit in two tomatoes. Insert a garlic clove into each slit.

2. Place all tomatoes and onions in a 3-qt. slow cooker.

3. Cut stems off jalapeños. (Remove seeds if you want a milder salsa.) Place jalapeños in the slow cooker.

4. Cover and cook on High for 2½–3 hours or until vegetables are softened. Some may brown slightly. Cool at least 2 hours with the lid off.

5. In a blender, combine the tomato mixture, cilantro, and salt if you wish. Cover and process until blended.

6. Refrigerate leftovers.

Serving suggestion:

Garnish with cilantro and jalapeño.

TIP

Wear disposable gloves when cutting hot peppers; the oils can burn your skin. Avoid touching your face when you've been working with hot peppers.

Chili Cheese Dip

Hope Comerford
Clinton Township, MI

Makes 6 cups
Prep. Time: 1 hour and 15 minutes ⚜ *Cooking Time: 1–2 hours* ⚜ *Ideal slow-cooker size: 2- or 3-qt.*

1½ cups raw cashews

water

1 orange bell pepper, chopped

1 cup almond milk

2 tsp. chili powder

¼ cup nutritional yeast

¼ cup onion, minced

2 Tbsp. vegan taco seasoning

2 (15-oz.) cans pinto beans, drained and rinsed

12 oz. fresh salsa

2 Tbsp. fresh cilantro, finely chopped

1. Soak the cashews in water for 1 hour then drain the water.

2. Place the cashews into a blender with bell peppers, almond milk, chili powder, and nutritional yeast. Blend until smooth, thick, and creamy.

3. Place the blended mixture into the crock with the remaining ingredients and stir.

4. Cover and heat on Low for 1–2 hours, or until heated through.

Bean Cheese Dip

Wafi Brandt
Manheim, PA

Diana Kampnich
Croghan, NY

Makes 3 cups

Prep. Time: 5–10 minutes ❧ *Cooking Time: 1–2 hours* ❧ *Ideal slow-cooker size: 3-qt.*

2 cups canned kidney beans, drained
and mashed

1 cup salsa

1 cup vegan shredded cheddar cheese

¼ tsp. garlic powder

½ tsp. chili powder

¼ tsp. ground coriander

½ tsp. ground cumin

tortilla chips

1. Mix all ingredients except chips in slow cooker.

2. Cook on Low 1–2 hours until hot through.

3. Serve with tortilla chips.

Variations:

Omit spices. Use whole pinto beans instead of mashed kidney beans. Add 8 oz. vegan cream cheese.

—Diana Kampnich

TIP

Mash the beans with the bottom of a cup or in a food processor.

Hummus

Colleen Heatwole
Burton, MI

Makes 8 servings
Prep. Time: 15 minutes ⚶ Cooking Time: 40 minutes ⚶ Setting: Manual or Bean
Pressure: High ⚶ Release: Natural

1 cup dry garbanzo beans (chickpeas)

4 cups water

2 Tbsp. fresh lemon juice

¼ cup chopped onion

3 cloves garlic, minced

½ cup tahini (sesame paste)

2 tsp. cumin

2 tsp. olive oil

pinch cayenne pepper

½ tsp. salt

1. Place garbanzo beans and 4 cups water into inner pot of Instant Pot. Secure lid and make sure vent is set to sealing.

2. Cook garbanzo beans and water for 40 minutes using the Manual high pressure setting.

3. When cooking time is up, let the pressure release naturally.

4. Test the garbanzos. If still firm, cook using slow-cooker function until they are soft.

5. Drain the garbanzo beans, but save ½ cup of the cooking liquid.

6. Combine the garbanzos, lemon juice, onion, garlic, tahini, cumin, oil, pepper, and salt in a blender or food processor.

7. Purée until smooth, adding chickpea liquid as needed to thin the purée. Taste and adjust seasonings accordingly.

Candied Pecans

Hope Comerford
Clinton Township, MI

Makes 10 servings
Prep. Time: 5 minutes   ❧   Cooking Time: 15 minutes   ❧   Setting: Sauté and Mannual
Pressure: High   ❧   Release: Manual

4 cups raw pecans

⅔ cup maple syrup

½ cup plus 1 Tbsp. water, divided

1 tsp. vanilla extract

1 tsp. cinnamon

¼ tsp. nutmeg

⅛ tsp. ground ginger

⅛ tsp. sea salt

1. Place the raw pecans, maple syrup, 1 Tbsp. water, vanilla, cinnamon, nutmeg, ground ginger, and sea salt into the inner pot of the Instant Pot.

2. Press the Sauté button on the Instant Pot and sauté the pecans and other ingredients until the pecans are soft.

3. Pour in the ½ cup water and secure the lid to the locked position. Set the vent to sealing.

4. Press Manual and set the Instant Pot for 15 minutes.

5. Preheat the oven to 350°F.

6. When cooking time is up, turn off the Instant Pot then do a quick release.

7. Spread the pecans onto a greased, lined baking sheet.

8. Bake the pecans for 5 minutes or less in the oven, checking on them frequently so they do not burn.

Curried Almonds

Barbara Aston
Ashdown, AR

Makes 64 servings (1 Tbsp. each)
Prep. Time: 5 minutes ⚶ *Cooking Time: 3½–4½ hours* ⚶ *Ideal slow-cooker size: 3-qt.*

2 Tbsp. coconut oil

1 Tbsp. curry powder

½ tsp. sea salt

⅛ tsp. turmeric

⅛ tsp. paprika

⅛ tsp. onion powder

⅛ tsp. garlic powder

⅛ tsp. sugar

1 lb. blanched almonds

1. Combine coconut oil with spices.

2. Pour over almonds in slow cooker. Mix to coat well.

3. Cover. Cook on Low 2–3 hours. Turn to High. Uncover cooker and cook 1–1½ hours.

4. Serve warm or at room temperature.

Sweet-and-Hot Mixed Nuts

Hope Comerford
Clinton Township, MI

Makes 22 servings (about ¼ cup each)
Prep. Time: 15 minutes   ♣   Cooking Time: 2 hours
Cooling Time: 1 hour   ♣   Ideal slow-cooker size: 2- or 3-qt.

I cup unsalted cashews
I cup unsalted almonds
I cup unsalted pecans
I cup unsalted, shelled pistachios
½ cup maple syrup
⅓ cup melted coconut oil
I tsp. ground ginger
½ tsp. sea salt
½ tsp. cinnamon
¼ tsp. ground cloves
¼ tsp. cayenne pepper

1. Spray crock with nonstick spray.

2. Place nuts in the crock and combine them with all the remaining ingredients, making sure all nuts are coated evenly.

3. Before covering the crock, place a piece of paper towel or thin dishtowel under the lid. Cook on Low for 1 hour and then stir the nuts. At 2 hours, stir again and then lay them on a parchment paper-lined cookie sheet. Let them cool for 1 hour.

4. Serve or store any remaining nuts in a covered container for up to 3 weeks.

 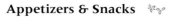

Insta Popcorn

Hope Comerford
Clinton Township, MI

Makes 5–6 servings
Prep. Time: 1 minute ⚘ *Cooking Time: about 5 minutes* ⚘ *Setting: Sauté*

2 Tbsp. coconut oil

½ cup popcorn kernels

¼ cup vegan butter, melted

sea salt, to taste

1. Set the Instant Pot to Sauté.

2. Melt the coconut oil in the inner pot, then add the popcorn kernels and stir.

3. Press Adjust to bring the temperature up to high.

4. When the corn starts popping, secure the lid on the Instant Pot.

5. When you no longer hear popping, turn off the Instant Pot, remove the lid, and pour the popcorn into a bowl.

6. Season the popcorn with the melted vegan butter and sea salt to your liking.

Soups, Stews & Chilies

Slow Cooker Tomato Soup

Becky Fixel
Grosse Pointe Farms, MI

Makes 8 servings
Prep. Time: 15 minutes ⚘ *Cooking Time: 6 hours* ⚘ *Ideal slow-cooker size: 6-qt.*

6–8 cups chopped fresh tomatoes
1 medium onion, chopped
2 tsp. minced garlic
1 tsp. basil
½ tsp. pepper
½ tsp. sea salt
½ tsp. red pepper flakes
2 Tbsp. vegetable bouillon
1 cup water
¾ cup dairy-free half-and-half

1. Combine your tomatoes, onion, spices, vegetable bouillon, and 1 cup of water in your slow cooker.

2. Cover and cook on Low for 6 hours.

3. Add in your ¾ cup dairy-free half-and-half and combine all ingredients with an immersion blender. Serve hot.

Unstuffed Cabbage Soup

Colleen Heatwole
Burton, MI

Makes 4–6 servings
Prep. Time: 10 minutes ❧ Cooking Time: 10–20 minutes ❧ Setting: Sauté and Manual
Pressure: High ❧ Release: Natural then Manual

2 Tbsp. coconut oil

1 medium onion, diced

2 cloves garlic, minced

1 small head cabbage, chopped, cored, cut into roughly 2-inch pieces

16 oz. meatless crumbles

6-oz. can tomato paste

32-oz. can diced tomatoes, with liquid

2 cups vegetable broth

1 ½ cups water

¾ cup white or brown rice

1–2 tsp. salt

½ tsp. black pepper

1 tsp. oregano

1 tsp. parsley

1. Melt coconut oil in the inner pot of the Instant Pot using Sauté function. Add onion and garlic and to sauté for 2 minutes, stirring frequently.

2. Add chopped cabbage and meatless crumbles.

3. On top of cabbage and meatless crumble, layer tomato paste, tomatoes with liquid, vegetable broth, water, rice, and spices.

4. Secure the lid and set vent to sealing. Using Manual setting, select 10 minutes if using white rice, 20 minutes if using brown rice.

5. When time is up, let the pressure release naturally for 10 minutes, then do a quick release.

Tofu and Vegetable Soup

Hope Comerford
Clinton Township, MI

Makes 4–6 servings
Prep. Time: 30 minutes ❧ Cooking Time: 6–7 hours ❧ Ideal slow-cooker size: 5-qt.

16 oz. diced extra-firm tofu, drained and pressed

2 celery ribs, diced

1 small yellow squash, diced

4 oz. sliced mushrooms

2 large carrots, diced

1 medium onion, chopped

2 Tbsp. garlic powder

1 Tbsp. onion powder

1 Tbsp. basil

½ tsp. no-salt seasoning

1 tsp. salt

black pepper, to taste

32 oz. vegetable chicken stock

1. Place the tofu, vegetables, and spices into the crock. Pour the vegetable stock over the top.

2. Cover and cook on Low for 6–7 hours, or until vegetables are tender.

Potato Leek Soup

Melissa Paskvan
Novi, MI

Makes 4–6 servings
Prep. Time: 20 minutes & Cooking Time: 6 hours & Ideal slow-cooker size: 6-qt.

3 large leeks, chopped (rinse leek well and include the tough tops)

5 medium Yukon Gold potatoes, chopped

2 cups gluten-free vegetable stock

2 cups water

2–3 bay leaves

½ head of cauliflower, broken up

3 stalks of celery, whole

¼ tsp pepper

salt, to taste

1. Place all of the ingredients in the slow cooker and put the tough tops of the leeks on the top.

2. Cover and cook on Low for 6 hours.

3. Remove tough leek tops, celery, and bay leaves. Either blend all the ingredients in a blender or use an immersion blender while in the crock and blend until very creamy. Salt to taste and add water if too thick for your liking.

Vegetable Soup with Rice

Hope Comerford
Clinton Township, MI

Makes 6–8 servings
Prep. Time: 30 minutes ♣ Cooking Time: 6½–7½ hours ♣ Ideal slow-cooker size: 3-qt.

32 oz. extra firm tofu, drained and pressed, then diced

1½ cups chopped carrots

1½ cups chopped red onion

2 Tbsp. garlic powder

1 Tbsp. onion powder

2 tsp. kosher salt (you can omit the salt if you're using regular stock rather than no-salt)

¼ tsp. celery seed

¼ tsp. paprika

⅛ tsp. pepper

1 dried bay leaf

8 cups vegetable stock

1 cup fresh green beans

3 cups cooked rice

1. Place tofu into the bottom of crock, then add the remaining ingredients, except green beans and rice.

2. Cover and cook on Low for 6–7 hours.

3. 30 minutes before you're ready to serve, add in green beans. Cover and cook another 30 minutes.

4. To serve, place approximately ½ cup of the cooked rice into each bowl and ladle soup over top of the rice.

Black Bean Soup

Colleen Heatwole
Burton, MI

Makes 4–6 servings
Prep. Time: 20 minutes ⚶ Cooking Time: 25 minutes (unless beans have been soaked)
Setting: Sauté and Bean/Chili ⚶ Pressure: High ⚶ Release: Natural

2 Tbsp. coconut oil

I cup coarsely chopped onion

2 cups dry black beans, cleaned of debris and rinsed

6 cups vegetable broth

3 cloves garlic, minced

½ tsp. paprika

⅛ tsp. red pepper flakes

2 large bay leaves

I tsp. cumin

2 tsp. oregano

½ tsp. salt (more if desired)

dairy-free yogurt, dairy-free sour cream for garnish, optional

1. Heat the oil in the inner pot of the Instant Pot with the Sauté function. Add onion and sauté 2 minutes.

2. Add remaining ingredients except garnishes, and stir well.

3. Secure lid and make sure vent is at sealing, then set to Bean/Chili for 25 minutes.

4. After time is up let pressure release naturally.

5. Remove bay leaves and serve with desired garnishes.

Hearty Bean and Vegetable Soup

Jewel Showalter
Landisville, PA

Makes 8–10 servings
Prep. Time: 20–25 minutes ♣ *Cooking Time: 6–8 hours* ♣ *Ideal slow-cooker size: 5-qt.*

2 medium onions, sliced
2 cloves garlic, minced
2 Tbsp. olive oil
8 cups vegetable broth
1 small head cabbage, chopped
2 large red potatoes, chopped
2 cups chopped celery
2 cups chopped carrots
4 cups corn
2 tsp. dried basil
1 tsp. dried marjoram
¼ tsp. dried oregano
1 tsp. salt
½ tsp. pepper
2 (15-oz.) cans navy beans, drained, rinsed

1. Sauté onions and garlic in oil in skillet. Transfer to large slow cooker.

2. Add remaining ingredients. Mix together well.

3. Cover. Cook on Low 6–8 hours.

Zucchini Stew

Colleen Heatwole
Burton, MI

Makes 6 servings
Prep. Time: 30 minutes ⚬ *Cooking Time: 4–6 hours* ⚬ *Ideal slow-cooker size: 6-qt.*

16 oz. meatless Italian-style sausage, sliced

2 stalks celery, diced

2 medium green bell peppers, diced

1 medium onion, chopped

2 (28-oz.) cans diced tomatoes

2 lb. zucchini, cut into ½-inch slices

2 cloves garlic, minced

1 tsp. sugar

1 tsp. dried oregano

1 tsp. Italian seasoning

1 tsp. sea salt, optional (taste first)

6 Tbsp. nutritional yeast flakes, optional

1. Sauté sausage in hot skillet until brown, about 5 minutes.

2. Mix celery, bell peppers, and onion into cooked sausage and cook and stir until they are softened, 10–12 minutes.

3. Combine with remaining ingredients, except nutritional yeast flakes, and add to slow cooker.

4. Cook on Low 4–6 hours. Garnish each serving with 1 Tbsp. nutritional yeast flakes if desired.

Tuscan Bean Soup

Jean Turner
Williams Lake, BC

Makes 4–6 servings

Prep. Time: 15 minutes ⚶ *Cooking Time: 2 hours* ⚶ *Ideal slow-cooker size: 4-qt.*

2 (14-oz.) cans chopped crushed tomatoes with herbs

1⅔ cups warm water

salt and pepper, to taste

2 cups Tuscan or curly kale, roughly shredded or chopped

14-oz. can cannellini beans or white beans, rinsed and drained

4 Tbsp. extra-virgin olive oil

1. Combine tomatoes, warm water, salt, pepper, and kale in slow cooker.

2. Cook on High for 1 hour.

3. Add beans. Cook on High another hour.

4. Place soup into bowls and drizzle each bowl with a little olive oil. Serve with warm crusty bread for dipping.

Tofu Tortilla Soup

Becky Fixel
Grosse Pointe Farms, MI

Makes 10–12 servings
Prep. Time: 5 minutes ⚬ *Cooking Time: 4–6 hours* ⚬ *Ideal slow-cooker size: 5-qt.*

16 oz. meatless crumbles

32 oz. vegetable stock

14 oz. vegan verde sauce

10-oz. can diced tomatoes with lime juice

15-oz. can sweet corn, drained

1 Tbsp. minced garlic

1 small onion, diced

1 Tbsp. chili pepper

½ tsp. fresh ground pepper

½ tsp. salt

½ tsp. oregano

1 Tbsp. dried jalapeño slices

1. Add all ingredients to your slow cooker.

2. Cook on Low for 4–6 hours.

Serving suggestion:

Top with a dollop of non-dairy Greek-style yogurt, shredded vegan cheese, fresh jalapeños, or fresh cilantro.

Taco Bean Soup

Colleen Heatwole
Burton, MI
Makes 8–10 servings
Prep. Time: 15 minutes   ⚶   Cooking Time: 4–6 hours   ⚶   Ideal slow-cooker size: 6-qt.

1 large onion, chopped

1 Tbsp. olive oil

16 oz. meatless crumbles

14-oz. can pinto beans, undrained

15-oz. can black beans, undrained

15-oz. can kidney beans, undrained

2 (14½-oz.) cans peeled and diced tomatoes or 1 qt. fresh tomatoes

15-oz. can low-sodium tomato sauce

4-oz. can diced green chilies

1 pkg. vegan taco seasoning

15-oz. can whole-kernel corn, undrained

1. Brown onion in skillet with olive oil.

2. Place onion in slow cooker along with all the other ingredients.

3. Cook on Low 4–6 hours.

Serving suggestion:

Serve with dairy-free sour cream, grated vegan cheese, and tortilla chips.

TIPS

- You can skip browning the onions if you are short on time.

- Any beans can be used in this recipe. You can keep frozen beans that you have cooked on hand and just use a combination.

Chickpea Tortilla Soup

Hope Comerford
Clinton Township, MI

Makes 4–6 servings
Prep. Time: 5 minutes & Cooking Time: 4–6 hours & Ideal slow-cooker size: 4-qt.

2 (15-oz.) cans garbanzo beans
(chickpeas), drained

2 (14½-oz.) cans petite diced tomatoes

6 cups vegetable stock

1 onion, chopped

4-oz. can diced green chilies

1 tsp. cilantro

3–4 fresh cloves garlic, minced

1 tsp. sea salt

1 tsp. pepper

1 tsp. cumin

1 tsp. paprika

1. Place all ingredients in slow cooker.

2. Cover and cook on Low for 4–6 hours.

Serving suggestion:

Serve with a small dollop of vegan Greek yogurt, a little vegan shredded cheddar, and some baked blue corn tortilla chips.

"Meatball" and Pasta Soup

Michele Ruvola
Vestal, NY

Makes 4–5 servings
Prep. Time: 10 minutes ⚜ *Cooking Time: 9 minutes* ⚜ *Setting: Manual*
Pressure: High ⚜ *Release: Manual*

1 cup diced carrots
½ cup diced celery
¾ cup diced onion
12.7-oz. bag frozen meatless meatballs
1½ cups ditalini pasta
40 oz. vegetable broth
1 tsp. salt
½ tsp. black pepper
2 Tbsp. diced parsley
2 Tbsp. diced green onions

1. Place all ingredients, except the parsley and green onions, in the inner pot of the Instant Pot and stir.

2. Secure the lid, make sure vent is set to sealing, then put on Manual function, set to high pressure, for 9 minutes.

3. Use quick release to release pressure, then stir.

4. Top with parsley and green onions.

Enchilada Soup

Melissa Paskvan
Novi, MI

Makes 6–8 servings
Prep. Time: 5 minutes   ⚘   Cooking Time: 6–8 hours   ⚘   Ideal slow-cooker size: 6-qt.

14½-oz. can of diced tomatoes with green chilies or chipotles

12-oz. jar vegan enchilada sauce

4 cups vegetable broth

1 small onion, chopped

3 cups tri-colored peppers, sliced

10-oz. pkg. frozen corn

1 cup water

½ cup uncooked quinoa

1. Add all ingredients to slow cooker.

2. Cover and cook on Low for 6–8 hours.

Serving suggestion:

Garnish with sliced jalapeños and pepitas.

TIP
You could add some meatless crumbles to this to give it a bit more protein if desired.

Minestrone

Bernita Boyts
Shawnee Mission, KS

Makes 8–10 servings
Prep. Time: 15 minutes ⚜ *Cooking Time: 4–9 hours* ⚜ *Ideal slow-cooker size: 3½- to 4-qt.*

1 large onion, chopped

4 carrots, sliced

3 stalks celery, sliced

2 cloves garlic, minced

1 Tbsp. olive oil

6-oz. can tomato paste

2 cups vegetable broth

24-oz. can pinto beans, drained, rinsed

10-oz. pkg. frozen green beans

2–3 cups chopped cabbage

1 medium zucchini, sliced

8 cups water

2 Tbsp. parsley

2 Tbsp. Italian seasoning

1 tsp. sea salt, or more, to taste

½ tsp. pepper

¾ cup dry acini di pepe (small round pasta)

nutritional yeast flakes, optional

1. Sauté onion, carrots, celery, and garlic in oil in skillet until tender. Add to slow cooker.

2. Combine all other ingredients, except pasta and nutritional yeast flakes, in slow cooker.

3. Cover. Cook 4–5 hours on High or 8–9 hours on Low.

4. Add pasta 1 hour before cooking is complete.

5. Top individual servings with nutritional yeast flakes, if desired.

Asian Noodle Soup

Carol Eveleth
Cheyenne, WY

Makes 4–6 servings
Prep. Time: 15 minutes ⚶ Cooking Time: 10 minutes ⚶ Setting: Manual
Pressure: High ⚶ Release: Manual

16 oz. extra-firm tofu, drained, pressed and diced

1 medium onion, chopped

3 stalks celery, sliced

1 bay leaf

6 cups vegetable broth

2 medium carrots, thinly sliced

1 medium red bell pepper, coarsely chopped

8 oz. rice noodles

4 cloves garlic, minced

2 Tbsp. liquid aminos

2 Tbsp. finely chopped fresh ginger

½ tsp. sage

½ tsp. black pepper

3 cups shredded cabbage

3–4 Tbsp. rice vinegar

1. Put all ingredients into the inner pot of the Instant Pot.

2. Secure the lid on the pot. Close the pressure-release valve. Select Manual and cook at high pressure for 10 minutes.

3. When cooking is complete, use a quick release to depressurize. Press Cancel to turn the pot off.

Vegetarian Split Pea Soup

Colleen Heatwole
Burton, MI

Makes 6 servings
Prep. Time: 30 minutes   &   *Cooking Time: 5–6 hours*   &   *Ideal slow-cooker size: 6-qt.*

1 lb. split peas, sorted and rinsed

2 qt. vegetable broth

2 cups water

1 large onion, chopped

2 cloves garlic, minced

3 ribs celery, chopped

3 medium carrots, chopped finely

2 bay leaves

1 tsp. kosher salt

1 tsp. black pepper

1. Combine all ingredients and add to slow cooker.

2. Cover and cook on Low 5–6 hours. Remove bay leaves and serve, or blend with an immersion blender for a creamy texture.

Brown Lentil Soup

Colleen Heatwole
Burton, MI

Makes 3–5 servings
Prep. Time: 15 minutes ♣ Cooking Time: 20 minutes ♣ Setting: Sauté and Manual
Pressure: High ♣ Release: Manual

1 medium onion, chopped
1 Tbsp. olive oil
1 medium carrot, diced
2 cloves garlic, minced
1 small bay leaf
1 lb. brown lentils
5 cups vegetable broth
1 tsp. salt
¼ tsp. ground black pepper
½ tsp. lemon juice

1. Using the Sauté function, sauté the chopped onion in oil in the inner pot of the Instant Pot about 2 minutes, or until it starts to soften.

2. Add diced carrot and sauté 3 minutes more until it begins to soften. Stir frequently or it will stick.

3. Add garlic and sauté 1 more minute.

4. Add bay leaf, lentils, and broth to pot.

5. Secure the lid and make sure vent is at sealing. Using Manual setting, select 14 minutes and cook on high pressure.

6. When cooking time is up, do a quick release of the pressure.

7. Discard bay leaf.

8. Stir in salt, pepper, and lemon juice, then adjust seasonings to taste.

Lentil Soup with Lemon

Heidi Wood
Vacaville, CA

Makes 6 servings
Prep. Time: 10 minutes ⚬ *Cooking Time: 8 hours* ⚬ *Ideal slow-cooker size: 5-qt.*

⅓ cup olive oil
2 large sweet onions, chopped
4 cloves garlic, minced
2 tsp. ground cumin
½ tsp. salt
½ tsp. freshly ground black pepper
¼ tsp. chili powder
8 cups vegetable broth
2 cups dry red lentils
2 large carrots, diced
2 Tbsp. tomato paste
4 Tbsp. lemon juice
1 cup chopped fresh cilantro
non-dairy plain yogurt, optional

1. Heat olive oil in a skillet over medium-high heat. Stir in the onions and garlic, and cook until the onion is golden brown, about 5 minutes.

2. Add the browned onions and garlic to the crock along with the cumin, salt, pepper, chili powder, broth, lentils, carrots, and tomato paste. Stir.

3. Cover and cook on Low for 8 hours.

4. Just before serving, stir lemon juice into the pot of soup.

5. Ladle soup into bowls. Serve cilantro on the side to be added as a garnish. It is also good with a dollop of plain non-dairy yogurt for a slightly different taste.

Serving suggestion:

This is delightful served with a crusty loaf of vegan whole grain bread and a green salad.

Butternut Squash Soup

Colleen Heatwole
Burton, MI

Makes 4 servings
Prep. Time: 30 minutes & Cooking Time: 15 minutes & Setting: Sauté and Manual
Pressure: High & Release: Manual

2 Tbsp. vegan butter

1 large onion, chopped

2 cloves garlic, minced

1 tsp. thyme

½ tsp. sage

salt and pepper, to taste

2 large butternut squash, peeled, seeded, and cubed (about 4 pounds)

4 cups vegetable stock

1. In the inner pot of the Instant Pot, melt the vegan butter using sauté function.

2. Add onion and garlic and cook until soft, 3 to 5 minutes.

3. Add thyme and sage and cook another minute. Season with salt and pepper.

4. Stir in butternut squash and add vegetable stock.

5. Secure the lid and make sure vent is at sealing. Using Manual setting, cook squash and seasonings 10 minutes, using high pressure.

6. When time is up, do a quick release of the pressure.

7. Purée the soup in a food processor or use immersion blender right in the inner pot. If soup is too thick, add more stock. Adjust salt and pepper as needed.

Creamy Butternut Squash Soup

Hope Comerford
Clinton Township, MI

Makes 4–6 servings
Prep. Time: 20 minutes ❦ Cooking Time: 8 hours ❦ Ideal slow-cooker size: 3-qt.

1½-lb. butternut squash, peeled and cut into 1-inch chunks

1 small onion, quartered

1 carrot, cut into 1-inch chunks

1 small sweet potato, cut into 1-inch chunks

¼ tsp. cinnamon

⅛ tsp. nutmeg

½ tsp. sugar

¼ tsp. salt

⅛ tsp. pepper

⅛ tsp. ginger

3 cups vegetable stock

1 cup dairy-free half-and-half

1. Place the butternut squash, onion, carrot, and sweet potato pieces into your crock.

2. Sprinkle the contents of the crock with the cinnamon, nutmeg, sugar, salt, pepper, and ginger. Pour the stock over the top.

3. Cover and cook on Low for 8 hours, or until the vegetables are soft.

4. Using an immersion blender, blend the soup until smooth.

5. Remove ¼ cup of the soup and mix it with 1 cup of the dairy-free half-and-half. Pour this into the crock and mix until well combined.

Butternut Squash Soup with Thai Gremolata

Andy Wagner
Quarryville, PA

Makes 4–6 servings
Prep. Time: 25 minutes ⚘ *Cooking Time: 2–5 hours* ⚘ *Ideal slow-cooker size: 3½- or 4-qt.*

2 lb. butternut squash, peeled and cut into 1-inch pieces

2 cups vegetable broth

14-oz. can unsweetened coconut milk

¼ cup minced onions

1 Tbsp. brown sugar, packed

1 Tbsp. liquid aminos

½–1 tsp. crushed red pepper

2 Tbsp. lime juice

lime wedges, optional

Thai Gremolata:

½ cup chopped fresh basil or cilantro

½ cup chopped peanuts

1 Tbsp. finely shredded lime peel

1. In a 3½- or 4-qt. slow cooker, stir together squash, broth, coconut milk, onions, brown sugar, liquid aminos, and crushed red pepper.

2. Cover and cook on Low for 4–5 hours or on High for 2–2½ hours.

3. Meanwhile, assemble the Thai Gremolata. Mix together basil, peanuts, and lime peel. Set aside.

4. Use an immersion or stand blender to carefully blend soup until completely smooth.

5. Stir in lime juice. Ladle into bowls and top with Thai Gremolata. If you wish, serve with lime wedges.

Vegan Chili

Denise Nolt
Fleetwood, PA

Makes 8 servings
Prep. Time: 10 minutes ♣ *Cooking Time: 2–3 hours* ♣ *Ideal slow-cooker size: 5-qt.*

28-oz. can crushed tomatoes

15-oz. can light or dark kidney beans,
rinsed and drained

15-oz. can black beans, rinsed and
drained

15-oz. can chili beans

11-oz. can Mexican-style corn

8-oz. can crushed pineapple

1 green bell pepper, diced

1 red bell pepper, diced

1 yellow bell pepper, diced

1 orange bell pepper, diced

1 medium red onion, diced

1 hot chili pepper, diced, optional

garlic, to taste

paprika, to taste

cayenne pepper, to taste

chili powder, to taste

1. Combine all ingredients in slow cooker.

2. Cook on High 2–3 hours or until vegetables are as soft as you like them. Serve with tortilla chips.

Black Bean Chili

Kenda Autumn
San Francisco, CA

Makes 6–8 servings
Prep. Time: 15 minutes   ⚜   Cooking Time: 8 hours   ⚜   Ideal slow-cooker size: 5-qt.

1 Tbsp. olive oil

1 medium onion, chopped

1 tsp. ground cumin

1 tsp. ground coriander

1 Tbsp. chili powder

1 tsp. garam masala

16-oz. can black beans, rinsed and drained

14-oz. can diced tomatoes

1 sweet potato, cubed

2 cups cubed butternut squash

1 cup corn

1. Heat oil in saucepan. Brown onion, cumin, coriander, chili powder, and garam masala.

2. Transfer to slow cooker.

3. Add beans, tomatoes, sweet potato, butternut squash, and corn.

4. Cook on Low 8 hours.

TIP

Use this recipe as a starting point for chili. You can add other vegetables in step 3 that you have on hand, such as red bell pepper and mushrooms.

White Bean Chili

Hope Comerford
Clinton Township, MI

Makes 6–8 servings
Prep. Time: 15 minutes & Cooking Time: 8–10 hours & Ideal slow-cooker size: 5-qt.

16. oz extra firm tofu, drained and pressed, diced

½ cup dry navy beans, soaked overnight, drained, and rinsed

½ cup dry great northern beans, soaked overnight, drained, and rinsed

½ cup chopped carrots

1½ cups chopped onion

2 (14½-oz.) cans petite diced tomatoes

5 cloves garlic, minced

6-oz. can tomato paste

1 Tbsp. cumin

1 Tbsp. chili powder

1 tsp. salt

¼ tsp. pepper

8 cups vegetable stock

1. Place all ingredients into the crock and stir to mix well.

2. Cover and cook on Low for 8–10 hours.

Southwestern Chili

Colleen Heatwole
Burton, MI

Makes 12 servings
Prep. Time: 30 minutes ⚶ *Cooking Time: 6–8 hours* ⚶ *Ideal slow-cooker size: 6- or 7-qt.*

32-oz. can whole tomatoes

15-oz. jar salsa

15-oz. can vegetable broth

1 cup barley

3 cups water

1 tsp. chili powder

1 tsp. ground cumin

15-oz. can black beans

15-oz. can whole kernel corn

24 oz. meatless crumbles

1 cup vegan shredded cheese, optional

non-dairy sour cream, optional

1. Combine all ingredients in slow cooker except for vegan cheese and non-dairy sour cream.

2. Cover and cook on Low for 6–8 hours.

3. Serve with vegan cheese and non-dairy sour cream on each bowl, if desired.

White Chili

Rebecca Plank Leichty
Harrisonburg, VA

Makes 6–8 servings
Prep. Time: 15 minutes   Cooking Time: 4–10 hours   Ideal slow-cooker size: 5-qt.

15-oz. can chickpeas, or garbanzo beans, drained, rinsed

15-oz. can small northern beans, drained, rinsed

15-oz. can pinto beans, drained, rinsed

1 qt. frozen corn, or 2 1-lb. bags frozen corn

2 Tbsp. minced onions

1 red bell pepper, diced

3 tsp. minced garlic

3 tsp. ground cumin

½ tsp. salt

½ tsp. dried oregano

4 cups vegetable broth

1. Combine all ingredients in slow cooker.

2. Cover. Cook on Low 8–10 hours or on High 4–5 hours.

Serving suggestion:

Add a spoonful of salsa and a sprinkle of vegan cheese to each bowl of chili.

TIP
For more zip, add 2 tsp. chili powder, or one or more chopped jalapeño peppers, to Step 1.

Our Favorite Chili

Ruth Shank
Gridley, IL

Makes 10–12 servings
Prep. Time: 5 minutes ⚜ *Cooking Time: 6–7 hours* ⚜ *Ideal slow-cooker size: 5-qt.*

32 oz. meatless crumbles

¼ cup chopped onions

I stalk celery, chopped

extra-virgin olive oil, optional

29-oz. can stewed tomatoes

2 (15½-oz.) cans red kidney beans, drained, rinsed

2 (16-oz.) cans vegan chili beans, undrained

½ cup ketchup

I ½ tsp. lemon juice

2 tsp. vinegar

I tsp. brown sugar

I ½ tsp. kosher salt

I tsp. Worcestershire sauce

½ tsp. garlic powder

½ tsp. dry mustard powder

I Tbsp. chili powder

2 (6-oz.) cans tomato paste

1. Place all ingredients in crock. Mix well.

2. Cover. Cook on Low 6–7 hours.

Serving suggestion:

Serve with chopped avocados.

Main Dishes

Mjadra (Lentils and Rice)

Hope Comerford,
Clinton Township, MI

Makes 4–6 servings

Prep. Time: 1 hour 20 minutes ♣ Cooking Time: 8 hours ♣ Ideal slow-cooker size: 3-qt.

½ cup olive oil

2 large sweet onions, chopped

1 cup dried lentils, rinsed

4 cups water

¼ cup lemon juice

⅛ tsp. pepper

1 tsp. salt

1 cup uncooked white rice

1. In a sauté pan on the stovetop, heat the olive oil over medium-high heat. Add the onions and let brown lightly. Reduce the heat to low and cover. Let the onions caramelize for at least 1 hour.

2. When the onions are done, add them and all of the remaining ingredients to the crock and stir.

3. Cover and cook for 8 hours on Low.

Serving suggestion:

Serve with pita bread or on a bed of lettuce.

Slow-Cooked Lentils and Rice

Reba Rhodes
Bridgewater, VA

Makes 4–6 servings
Prep. Time: 20 minutes   ❧   Cooking Time: 2–3 hours   ❧   Ideal slow-cooker size: 3-qt.

1 cup dry green lentils
½ cup uncooked long-grain rice
3 tsp. dried minced onions
2 tsp. olive oil
3 cups boiling water
1 tsp. instant vegetable bouillon
2 tsp. vegan Worcestershire sauce
½ tsp. salt
½ tsp. pepper
1 tsp. dried thyme
1½ cups sliced fresh mushrooms

1. Rinse lentils.

2. Combine lentils, rice, onions, and olive oil in skillet. Sauté until rice grains begin to turn golden.

3. Pour into a 3-qt. slow cooker.

4. Combine boiling water with bouillon, stirring until bouillon dissolves.

5. Add to cooker along with vegan Worcestershire sauce, salt, pepper, thyme, and mushrooms. Stir gently.

6. Cover. Cook on Low 2–3 hours until lentils and rice are tender.

Quinoa and Black Beans

Gloria Frey
Lebanon, PA

Makes 6–8 servings
Prep. Time: 15 minutes ⚜ *Cooking Time: 1½–3 hours* ⚜ *Ideal slow-cooker size: 4-qt.*

1 tsp. olive oil
1 onion, chopped
3 cloves garlic, chopped
1 red bell pepper, chopped
¾ cup uncooked quinoa
1½ cups vegetable broth
1 tsp. ground cumin
¼ tsp. cayenne pepper
salt and pepper, to taste
1 cup frozen corn
2 (15-oz.) cans black beans rinsed and drained
½ cup fresh cilantro, chopped

1. Sauté onion, garlic, and red bell pepper in oil in skillet until softened. Place in 4-qt. slow cooker.

2. Mix quinoa into it and cover with vegetable broth.

3. Season with cumin, cayenne pepper, salt, and pepper.

4. Cover. Cook on Low 1–2 hours until quinoa is done.

5. Stir frozen corn, beans, and cilantro into cooker and continue to cook on Low 30–60 minutes until heated through.

Tortellini with Broccoli

Susan Kasting
Jenks, OK

Makes 4 servings
Prep. Time: 10 minutes & Cooking Time: 2½–3 hours & Ideal slow-cooker size: 4-qt.

½ cup water
26-oz. jar pasta sauce, your favorite
1 Tbsp. Italian seasoning
9-oz. pkg. frozen vegan tortellini
16-oz. pkg. frozen broccoli florets

1. Grease interior of slow-cooker crock.

2. In a bowl, mix water, pasta sauce, and seasoning together.

3. Pour one-third of sauce into bottom of slow cooker. Top with all the tortellini.

4. Pour one-third of sauce over tortellini. Top with broccoli.

5. Pour remaining sauce over broccoli.

6. Cook on High 2½–3 hours, or until broccoli and pasta are tender but not mushy.

Mexican Rice and Beans

Helen Schlabach
Winesburg, OH

Makes 6–8 servings
Prep. Time: 10 minutes ⚶ Cooking Time: 2–3 hours ⚶ Ideal slow-cooker size: 4-qt.

15-oz. can black beans, rinsed and drained

10-oz. pkg. frozen whole-kernel corn

1 cup uncooked long-grain white or brown rice

16-oz. jar thick and chunky mild salsa

1 ½ cups vegetable juice cocktail

½ tsp. ground cumin

½ tsp. dried oregano

salt and pepper, to taste

¾ cup shredded vegan cheddar cheese

1. Combine ingredients, except vegan cheese, in greased 4-qt. slow cooker.

2. Cook, covered, on High for 2–3 hours, stirring once.

3. When rice is tender, sprinkle with vegan shredded cheddar cheese. Serve and enjoy!

Tofu and Vegetables

Donna Lantgen
Rapid City, SD

Makes 4 servings
Prep. Time: 25–30 minutes ♣ *Cooking Time: 6 hours* ♣ *Ideal slow-cooker size: 4- or 5-qt.*

16 oz. firm tofu, drained and crumbled

½ cup chopped onion

½ cup chopped celery

2 cups chopped bok choy

2 cups chopped Napa cabbage

½ cup pea pods, cut in half

¼ cup liquid aminos or coconut aminos

1. Combine all ingredients in slow cooker.

2. Cook on Low 6 hours.

Serving suggestion:

This is wonderful served on a bed of rice.

Spicy Orange Tofu

Sue Hamilton
Benson, AZ

Makes 3 servings
Prep. Time: 5 minutes ❧ *Cooking Time: 5 hours* ❧ *Ideal slow-cooker size: 3-qt.*

12½ oz. extra firm gluten-free tofu, drained and diced

1½ cups orange marmalade (natural or low-sugar is best)

1 tsp. powdered ginger

1 tsp. minced garlic

1 Tbsp. balsamic vinegar

1 tsp. vegan sriracha sauce, or to taste

12-oz. bag of mixed stir-fry vegetables

1. Place the drained tofu in the crock.

2. Mix together the marmalade, ginger, garlic, vinegar, and sriracha sauce. Pour over the tofu, but don't mix as it will break up the tofu.

3. Cover and cook on Low for 4 hours.

4. Add the stir-fry vegetables on top and cook for 1 hour longer.

Serving suggestion:

Serve over brown rice.

Thai Tempeh and Noodles

Vonnie Oyer
Hubbard, OR

Makes 4 servings
Prep. Time: 15 minutes & Cooking Time: 12 minutes & Setting: Manual then Slow Cook
Pressure: High & Release: Manual

Thai peanut sauce:
¾ cup light coconut milk
½ cup peanut butter
2 Tbsp. sesame oil
¼ cup fresh lime juice
2 Tbsp. liquid aminos
1½ tsp. crushed red pepper flakes
1 Tbsp. seasoned rice vinegar
1 Tbsp. vegan "honey"
¼ tsp. ground ginger

32 oz. extra-firm tofu, drained and
pressed, diced
1½ cups vegetable broth
8 oz. dry rice noodles
5 oz. sugar snap peas (about 1½ cups)

1. Mix all the sauce ingredients in a blender. Makes 2 cups (this recipe uses 1 cup).

2. To the inner pot of the Instant Pot, add the tofu, 1 cup Thai peanut sauce, and broth.

3. Secure the lid and make sure vent is at sealing. Cook on Manual at high pressure for 2 minutes.

4. Do a quick release (manual) of the pressure. Remove the tofu from pot, leaving the sauce.

5. To the sauce, add the noodles and ensure all of the dry noodles are submerged in sauce. Top with the peas and replace the cover as quickly as possible.

6. Change the setting to Slow Cook and cook for 10 minutes, or until the noodles are soft but firm.

7. When cook time is up, remove the lid of the Instant Pot and give the noodles a good stir. Stir the tofu back into the inner pot with the noodles.

Mild Tempeh Curry with Coconut Milk

Brittney Horst
Lititz, PA

Makes 4–6 servings
Prep. Time: 30 minutes ⚘ Cooking Time: 7 minutes ⚘ Setting: Sauté and Manual
Pressure: High ⚘ Release: Natural

1 large onion, diced

6 cloves garlic, crushed

64 oz. extra-firm tofu, drained, pressed and diced

¼ cup coconut oil or avocado oil

½ tsp. black pepper

½ tsp. turmeric

½ tsp. paprika

¼ tsp. cinnamon

¼ tsp. cloves

¼ tsp. cumin

¼ tsp. ginger

½ tsp. salt

1 Tbsp. curry powder (more if you like more flavor)

½ tsp. chili powder

24-oz. can of diced or crushed tomatoes

13½-oz. can of coconut milk (I prefer a brand that has no unwanted ingredients, like guar gum or sugar)

1. Sauté onion, garlic, and tofu in oil, with Sauté setting in the inner pot of the Instant Pot.

2. Combine spices in a small bowl, then add to the inner pot.

3. Add tomatoes and coconut milk and stir.

4. Secure the lid and make sure vent is at sealing. Set to Manual mode (or Pressure Cook on newer models) for 2 minutes.

5. Let pressure release naturally (if you're crunched for time, you can do a quick release).

6. Serve with your favorite sides, and enjoy!

Serving suggestion:

Serve with rice and a side of veggies.

Asian Style Tempeh with Pineapple

Andrea Maher
Dunedin, FL

Makes 6 servings
Prep. Time: 10 minutes   Cooking Time: 6 hours   Ideal slow-cooker size: 5- or 6-qt.

24 oz. tempeh, sliced into strips

3 cups pineapple, cubed

¼ cup liquid aminos

1 Tbsp. brown sugar

½ cup chopped onion or 2 Tbsp. onion powder

1 cup vegetable stock

½ tsp. ground ginger

2 16-oz. bags frozen Szechuan mixed veggies or any mixed veggies

1. Add all ingredients except for frozen veggies to the slow cooker.

2. Cover and cook on Low for 6 hours.

3. Add frozen veggies in the last 1–2 hours.

Juicy Orange Tempeh

Andrea Maher
Dunedin, FL

Makes 6 servings
Prep. Time: 10 minutes ⚕ Cooking Time: 6 hours ⚕ Ideal slow-cooker size: 5- or 6-qt.

18–24 oz. tempeh, cut into strips
1 cup orange juice, no additives
¼ cup vegan "honey"
6 small oranges, peeled and sliced
¼ cup liquid aminos
6 cups broccoli slaw

1. Add all the ingredients to the slow cooker except the broccoli slaw.

2. Cover and cook on Low 6 hours.

3. Divide mixture between 6 mason jars.

4. Add 1 cup broccoli slaw to each mason jar.

5. Pour into a bowl when you're ready to eat!

Tempeh Chow Mein

Hope Comerford
Clinton Township, MI

Makes 6 servings
Prep. Time: 15–20 minutes ⚜ Cooking Time: 5½–6½ hours ⚜ Ideal slow-cooker size: 3- or 4-qt.

16 oz. tempeh, sliced into strips

2 cups water

2 medium onions, halved and sliced into half rings

2–3 cups chopped celery

1 tsp. kosher salt

¼ tsp. pepper

2 tsp. quick-cooking tapioca

¼ cup liquid aminos

¼ cup brown sugar

16-oz. can baby corn, drained

6½-oz. can bamboo shoots, drained

1 cup bean sprouts

1 red bell pepper, chopped into slivers

1 carrot, chopped into thin matchsticks

1. Place the tempeh in the crock with the water, onions, celery, salt, and pepper.

2. Cover and cook on Low for 4–5 hours.

3. At the end of the 4–5 hours, in a small bowl, mix together the tapioca, liquid aminos, and brown sugar. Set aside.

4. Place the baby corn, bamboo shoots, bean sprouts, red bell pepper, and carrot into the crock.

5. Pour the sauce you just made from the small bowl into the slow cooker. Stir.

6. Cover and cook on Low an additional 1½ hours.

Serving suggestion:

Serve over rice noodles.

Tempeh Broccoli

Anita Troyer
Fairview, MI

Makes 6 servings
Prep. Time: 15 minutes ❧ Cooking Time: 10 minutes ❧ Setting: Manual and Sauté
Pressure: High ❧ Release: Manual

1 Tbsp. oil

24 oz. tempeh, sliced into strips

¼ tsp. black pepper

½ cup diced onion

3 cloves garlic, minced

¾ cup vegetable broth

½ cup liquid aminos

¼ cup brown sugar

2 Tbsp. sesame oil

¼ tsp. red pepper flakes

1 lb. broccoli, chopped

3 Tbsp. water

3 Tbsp. cornstarch

1. Put oil into the inner pot of the Instant Pot and select Sauté. When oil begins to sizzle, brown the tempeh in several small batches. After browning, remove and put into another bowl. Season with black pepper.

2. Sauté onion in pot for 2 minutes. Add garlic and sauté another minute. Add vegetable broth, liquid aminos, brown sugar, sesame oil, and red pepper flakes. Stir to mix well. Add tempeh on top of it.

3. Secure lid and make sure vent is at sealing. Set on Manual at high pressure and set timer for 2 minutes.

4. After beep, turn cooker off and use quick pressure release. Remove lid.

5. In microwave bowl, steam the broccoli for 3 minutes or until desired doneness.

6. In a small bowl, stir together water and cornstarch. Add to pot and stir. Put on Sauté setting and stir some more. After mixture becomes thick, add broccoli and turn pot off.

Serving suggestion:

Serve over rice.

Four-Pepper Tempeh Steak

Renee Hankins
Narvon, PA

Makes 14 servings
Prep. Time: 30 minutes ❧ *Cooking Time: 5–6 hours* ❧ *Ideal slow-cooker size: 4- or 5-qt.*

1 yellow pepper, sliced into ¼-inch thick pieces

1 red pepper, sliced into ¼-inch thick pieces

1 orange pepper, sliced into ¼-inch thick pieces

1 green pepper, sliced into ¼-inch thick pieces

2 cloves garlic, sliced

2 large onions, sliced

1 tsp. ground cumin

½ tsp. dried oregano

1 bay leaf

48 oz. tempeh, cut into strips

salt, to taste

2 (14½-oz.) cans low-sodium diced tomatoes in juice

jalapeño chilies, sliced, optional

1. Place sliced bell peppers, garlic, onions, cumin, oregano, and bay leaf in slow cooker. Stir gently to mix.

2. Put tempeh slices on top of vegetable mixture. Season with salt.

3. Spoon tomatoes with juice over top. Sprinkle with jalapeño pepper slices if you wish. Do not stir.

4. Cover and cook on Low 5–6 hours, depending on your slow cooker. Remove bay leaf and serve.

Plant-Based Kielbasa and Cabbage

Mary Ann Lefever
Lancaster, PA

Makes 4 servings

Prep. Time: 10–15 minutes ⚬ *Cooking Time: 6–8 hours* ⚬ *Ideal slow-cooker size: 4- or 5-qt.*

16 oz. plant-based kielbasa sausage, cut into 4 chunks

4 large white potatoes, cut into chunks

1-lb. head green cabbage, shredded

1 qt. whole tomatoes (strained if you don't like seeds)

1 medium onion, thinly sliced, optional

1. Layer kielbasa, then potatoes, and then cabbage into slow cooker.

2. Pour tomatoes over top.

3. Top with sliced onion if you wish.

4. Cover. Cook on Low 6–8 hours, or until vegetables are as tender as you like them.

Swedish Cabbage Rolls

Jean Butzer
Batavia, NY

Pam Hochstedler
Kalona, IA

Makes 6 servings

Prep. Time: 25 minutes ❧ *Cooking Time: 7–9 hours* ❧ *Ideal slow-cooker size: 2- to 4-qt.*

1 Tbsp. ground flaxseed

3 Tbsp. water

12 large cabbage leaves

¼ cup dairy-free milk

¼ cup finely chopped onions

1 tsp. sea salt

¼ tsp. pepper

16 oz. meatless crumbles

1 cup cooked brown rice

8-oz. can low-sodium tomato sauce

1 Tbsp. brown sugar

1 Tbsp. lemon juice

1 tsp. vegan Worcestershire sauce

1. Mix the flaxseed with the water and set aside to thicken for approximately 3 minutes.

2. Immerse cabbage leaves in boiling water for about 3 minutes or until limp. Drain.

3. Combine flaxseed/water mixture, milk, onions, salt, pepper, meatless crumbles, and rice. Place about ¼ cup mixture in center of each leaf. Fold in sides and roll ends over mixture. Place in slow cooker.

4. Combine tomato sauce, brown sugar, lemon juice, and vegan Worcestershire sauce. Pour over cabbage rolls.

5. Cover. Cook on Low 7–9 hours.

Goulash

Janie Steele
Moore, OK

Makes 8–10 servings
Prep. Time: 5 minutes ⚮ Cooking Time: 6 hours ⚮ Ideal slow-cooker size: 5-qt.

1 lb. meatless crumbles
1 pkg. vegan taco seasoning
2 cups water
15-oz. can low-sodium diced tomatoes
15-oz. can low-sodium tomato sauce
15-oz. can whole-kernel corn, drained
salt and pepper, to taste
2 cups uncooked elbow macaroni

1. Mix all ingredients together in your slow cooker.

2. Cover and cook 6 hours on Low.

Insta Pasta a la Maria

Maria Shevlin
Sicklerville, NJ

Makes 6–8 servings
Prep. Time: 10–15 minutes ❧ *Cooking Time: 6 minutes* ❧ *Setting: Manual*
Pressure: High ❧ *Release: Manual*

32-oz. jar of vegan spaghetti sauce or 1 qt. of homemade

2 cups fresh chopped spinach

1 cup chopped mushrooms

16 oz. meatless crumbles

1 tsp. salt

½ tsp. black pepper

½ tsp. dried basil

¼ tsp. red pepper flakes

1 tsp. parsley flakes

13¼-oz. box pasta

3 cups water

1. Place the sauce in the bottom of the inner pot of the Instant Pot.

2. Add in the spinach, then the mushrooms.

3. Add the meatless crumbles on top of the veggies and sauce.

4. Add the seasonings and give it a stir to mix.

5. Add the box of pasta.

6. Add 3 cups of water.

7. Secure the lid and move vent to sealing. Set to Manual on high pressure for 6 minutes.

8. When cook time is up, release the pressure manually.

9. Remove the lid and stir to mix together.

Zucchini-Vegetable Pot

Edwina Stoltzfus
Narvon, PA

Makes 6 servings
Prep. Time: 40 minutes & Cooking Time: 5–6 hours & Ideal slow-cooker size: 3½- or 4-qt.

2 cups diced zucchini

2 ribs celery, chopped

¼ cup chopped green bell peppers

1 large onion, chopped

2 large tomatoes, chopped

¼ cup brown rice, uncooked

16 oz. meatless crumbles

¾ tsp. sea salt

¼ tsp. garlic powder

⅛ tsp. nutmeg

¼ tsp. black pepper

1 tsp. vegan Worcestershire sauce

1. Place vegetables in slow cooker. Top with rice and meatless crumbles.

2. Sprinkle seasonings over top and add vegan Worcestershire sauce.

3. Cover and cook on Low for 5–6 hours.

Sloppy Joes

Hope Comerford
Clinton Township, MI

Makes 15–18 servings
Prep. Time: 25 minutes   ⚬   *Cooking Time: 6–7 hours*   ⚬   *Ideal slow-cooker size: 6-qt.*

12 oz. meatless crumbles

12 oz. ground vegan sausage

½ large red onion, chopped

½ green bell pepper, chopped

8-oz. can low-sodium tomato sauce

½ cup water

½ cup ketchup

¼ cup tightly packed brown sugar

2 Tbsp. apple cider vinegar

2 Tbsp. yellow mustard

1 Tbsp. vegan Worcestershire sauce

1 Tbsp. chili powder

1 tsp. garlic powder

1 tsp. onion powder

¼ tsp. salt

¼ tsp. pepper

1. Brown the meatless crumbles and vegan sausage in a pan then place in the crock.

2. Mix together the remaining ingredients in the crock with the crumbles.

3. Cover and cook on Low for 6–7 hours.

Serving suggestion:

Serve on your favorite vegan hamburger buns.

Filled Acorn Squash

Teresa Martin
New Holland, PA

Makes 4 servings
Prep. Time: 20–30 minutes ⚘ Cooking Time: 5–11 hours ⚘ Ideal slow-cooker size: oval 7-qt.

2 medium acorn squash, about 1¼ lb. each

2 Tbsp. water

15-oz. can black beans, drained, rinsed

½ cup pine nuts, raw, or toasted if you have time

1 large tomato, coarsely chopped

2 green onions, thinly sliced

1 tsp. ground cumin

½ tsp. black pepper, divided

2 tsp. olive oil

½–¾ cup shredded vegan mozzarella cheese

1. Grease interior of slow cooker crock.

2. Place washed whole squashes in slow cooker. Spoon in water.

3. Cover and cook for 4–6 hours on High or 7–9 hours on Low, or until squashes are tender when you pierce them with a fork.

4. While squashes are cooking, mix together beans, pine nuts, tomato, green onions, cumin, and ¼ tsp. black pepper. Set aside.

5. Use sturdy tongs, or wear oven mitts to lift squashes out of cooker. Let cool until you can cut them in half and scoop out the seeds.

6. Brush cut sides and cavity of each squash half with olive oil.

7. Sprinkle all 4 cut sides with remaining black pepper.

8. Spoon heaping ½ cup of bean mixture into each halved squash, pressing down gently to fill cavity.

9. Return halves to slow cooker. Cover and cook on High another hour, or on Low another 2 hours, until vegetables are as tender as you like them and thoroughly hot.

10. Uncover and sprinkle with cheese just before serving. Put a filled half squash on each diner's plate.

Soybean Loaf

Linda Gebo
Plattsburgh, NY

Makes 4–6 servings
Prep. Time: 20–25 minutes ⚬ Cooking Time: 4 hours
Standing Time: 8 hours or overnight ⚬ Ideal slow-cooker size: 4-qt.

I cup dry soybeans, soaked overnight

I tsp. dried parsley

¼ tsp. garlic powder

½ tsp. salt, optional

¼ tsp. paprika

½ tsp. crumbled dried sage

I ½ cups water

3 ribs celery, diced

I onion, diced

2 pimientos, diced, optional

2.2-oz. can pitted olives, sliced in half

I Tbsp. liquid aminos

I Tbsp. nutritional yeast flakes

½ cup vegan bread crumbs

1. In blender, purée soybeans, parsley, garlic powder, salt, paprika, and sage in water.

2. Pour into bowl. Add celery, onion, pimientos if you wish, olives, liquid aminos, nutritional yeast flakes, and bread crumbs. Place in 4-qt. slow cooker.

3. Cook covered on High for 4 hours.

Big-Batch Puttanesca Sauce

Monica Wagner
Quarryville, PA

Makes 11 cups

Prep. Time: 30 minutes   ⚶   *Cooking Time: 4–10 hours*   ⚶   *Ideal slow-cooker size: 6-qt.*

½ cup pitted Kalamata olives, divided

3 (28-oz.) cans diced tomatoes, undrained

6 Tbsp. tomato paste

1 large onion, chopped

4 cloves garlic, minced

¼ cup snipped fresh Italian parsley

2 Tbsp. capers, drained

2 tsp. dried basil

¼ tsp. cayenne pepper

¼ tsp. salt

¼ tsp. ground black pepper

pasta, cooked

nutritional yeast flakes, optional

1. Chop ¼ cup Kalamata olives. Halve the other ¼ cup and set aside.

2. In 4- to 6-qt. slow cooker stir together undrained tomatoes, tomato paste, onion, garlic, chopped olives, snipped parsley, capers, basil, cayenne pepper, salt, and ground black pepper.

3. Cover. Cook on Low 8–10 hours or High for 4–5 hours.

4. Remove half of sauce, about 5½ cups. Freeze or set aside for additional meals.

5. Turn slow cooker to High. Add halved olives to sauce in cooker. Cover. Cook 5 minutes more or until heated through.

6. Serve over hot cooked pasta. Sprinkle with nutritional yeast flakes if you wish.

Fresh Veggie Lasagna

Deanne Gingrich
Lancaster, PA

Makes 4–6 servings
Prep. Time: 30 minutes ⚜ *Cooking Time: 4 hours* ⚜ *Ideal slow-cooker size: 4- or 5-qt.*

I Tbsp. flaxseed
3 Tbsp. water
I ½ cups shredded vegan mozzarella cheese
½ cup vegan ricotta cheese
⅓ cup nutritional yeast
I tsp. dried oregano
¼ tsp. garlic powder
3 cups vegan marinara sauce, divided
I medium zucchini, diced, divided
4 uncooked gluten-free lasagna noodles
4 cups fresh baby spinach, divided
I cup fresh mushrooms, sliced, divided

1. Grease interior of slow-cooker crock.

2. Mix together the flaxseed and water and set aside for approximately 3 minutes to thicken.

3. When the flaxseed mixture has thickened, combine it with the vegan mozzarella, vegan ricotta, nutritional yeast, oregano, and garlic powder. Set aside.

4. Spread ½ cup marinara sauce in crock.

5. Sprinkle with half the zucchini.

6. Spoon ⅓ of vegan cheese mixture over the zucchini.

7. Break 2 noodles into large pieces to cover vegan cheese layer.

8. Spread ½ cup marinara over noodles.

9. Top with half the spinach and then half the mushrooms.

10. Repeat layers, ending with vegan cheese mixture, and then sauce. Press layers down firmly.

11. Cover and cook on Low for 4 hours, or until vegetables are as tender as you like them and noodles are fully cooked.

12. Let stand 15 minutes so lasagna can firm up before serving.

Vegetable Stuffed Peppers

Shirley Hinh
Wayland, IA

Makes 8 servings
Prep. Time: 20 minutes & Cooking Time: 6–8 hours & Ideal slow-cooker size: 6-qt.

4 large green, red, or yellow bell peppers
½ cup brown rice
¼ cup minced onions
¼ cup black olives, sliced
2 tsp. liquid aminos
¼ tsp. black pepper
1 clove garlic, minced
28-oz. can low-sodium whole tomatoes
6-oz. can low-sodium tomato paste
15¼-oz. can kidney beans, drained, rinsed

1. Cut tops off peppers (reserve) and remove seeds. Stand peppers up in slow cooker.

2. Mix remaining ingredients in a bowl. Stuff peppers. (You'll have leftover filling.)

3. Place pepper tops back on peppers. Pour remaining filling over the stuffed peppers and work down in between the peppers.

4. Cover and cook on Low 6–8 hours, or until the peppers are done to your liking.

5. If you prefer, you may add ½ cup tomato juice if recipe is too dry.

6. Cut peppers in half and serve.

Uniquely Stuffed Peppers

Maria Shevlin
Sicklerville, NJ

Makes 4 servings
Prep. Time: 20–30 minutes ❧ *Cooking Time: 15 minutes* ❧ *Setting: Manual*
Pressure: High ❧ *Release: Manual*

4 red bell peppers

1 tsp. olive oil

½ onion, chopped

3 cloves garlic, minced

8 oz. meatless crumbles

8 oz. spicy meatless sausage crumbles

1 tsp. salt

½ tsp. black pepper

1 tsp. garlic powder

½ tsp. dried oregano

½ tsp. dried basil

1 medium zucchini, grated and water pressed out

½ cup vegan barbecue sauce

¼ cup quick oats

1 cup water or vegetable broth

1. Cut the stem part of the top off the bell peppers, remove seeds and membranes, and set aside.

2. Add olive oil, onion, and garlic to a pan. Cook till al dente.

3. Add in all meatless crumbles, and brown lightly.

4. Add in your seasonings, zucchini, and barbecue sauce.

5. Add in your oats.

6. Mix well to combine.

7. Stuff the filling inside each pepper—pack it in.

8. Add 1 cup of water or vegetable broth to the bottom of the inner pot of the Instant Pot.

9. Add the rack to the pot.

10. Arrange the stuffed peppers standing upright.

11. Lock lid, make sure vent is at sealing, and use the Manual setting to set for 15 minutes.

12. When cook time is up, release the pressure manually.

Bell Pepper Casserole

Janie Steele
Moore, OK

Makes 6 servings
Prep. Time: 10 minutes 🍃 Cooking Time: 10 minutes 🍃 Setting: Manual
Pressure: High 🍃 Release: Natural

16 oz. meatless crumbles

1 Tbsp. olive oil

¾ cup long-grain rice

3–4 bell peppers, diced (your choice of colors)

½ cup diced onion

6-oz. can diced chilies

14-oz. can diced tomatoes

24-oz. jar vegan marinara sauce

½ tsp. chili powder

1 tsp. seasoned salt

2–3 cloves garlic, minced

1. Using the Sauté function, sauté the meatless crumbles in the olive oil in inner pot of the Instant Pot.

2. Add in the peppers and onion, then turn the Instant Pot off by hitting the Cancel button.

3. Add the remaining ingredients. Do NOT stir.

4. Secure the lid and make sure vent is at sealing. Turn the Instant Pot on Manual for 10 minutes.

5. Let the pressure release naturally.

Homemade Spaghetti Sauce

Beverly Hummel
Fleetwood, PA

Makes 12 cups
Prep. Time: 20 minutes ❧ Cooking Time: 4–5 hours ❧ Ideal slow-cooker size: 6-qt.

4 qts. cherry tomatoes
I onion, minced
2 cloves garlic, minced
I Tbsp. olive oil
3 tsp. sugar
I tsp. dried rosemary
2 tsp. dried thyme
2 tsp. Italian herb seasoning
I tsp. salt
½ tsp. pepper
hot cooked spaghetti

1. Stem tomatoes, leaving the skins on. Blend until smooth in blender.

2. In a skillet, sauté onion and garlic in oil.

3. Add sauté to slow cooker. Add tomatoes, sugar, rosemary, thyme, Italian seasoning, salt, and pepper.

4. Simmer on Low in slow cooker until thickened, about 4–5 hours. Remove the lid for the final 30–60 minutes of cooking time if you'd like a thicker sauce.

5. Serve over spaghetti.

Cacciatore Spaghetti

Maria Shevlin
Sicklerville, NJ

Makes 6 servings
Prep. Time: 15–20 minutes   ♣   Cooking Time: 5 minutes   ♣   Setting: Sauté and Manual
Pressure: High   ♣   Release: Manual

1 tsp. olive oil

1 medium sweet onion, chopped

3 cloves garlic, minced

1 lb. meatless crumbles

32-oz. jar vegan spaghetti sauce, or 1 qt. homemade

1 tsp. salt

½ tsp. black pepper

½ tsp. oregano

½ tsp. dried basil

½ tsp. red pepper flakes

1 cup bell pepper strips, mixed colors if desired

1 cup diced mushrooms, diced

13¼-oz. box Dreamfield spaghetti

3 cups vegetable broth

1. Press the Sauté button on the Instant Pot and add the oil, onion, and garlic to the inner pot.

2. Add in the meatless crumbles.

3. Once meatless crumbles are slightly browned, add in the sauce and seasonings.

4. Add in the bell peppers and mushrooms and give it a stir to mix.

5. Add in the spaghetti—break it in half in order for it to fit in.

6. Add in the vegetable broth.

7. Lock lid, make sure the vent is at sealing, and set on Manual at high pressure for 6 minutes.

8. When cook time is up, manually release the pressure.

Spaghetti with No-Meat Sauce

Becky Fixel
Grosse Pointe Farms, MI

Makes 6–8 servings

Prep. Time: 5 minutes ⚜ *Cooking Time: 6 hours* ⚜ *Ideal slow-cooker size: 7-qt.*

2 Tbsp. olive oil

28-oz. can crushed tomatoes

28-oz. can tomato sauce

15-oz. can Italian stewed tomatoes

6-oz. can tomato paste

2–3 Tbsp. basil

2 Tbsp. oregano

2 Tbsp. brown sugar

2 Tbsp. garlic paste (or 2 medium cloves, peeled and minced)

32. oz meatless crumbles

1. Pour olive oil in the crock. Use a paper towel to rub it all around the inside.

2. Add all ingredients to crock. Mix.

3. Cover and cook on Low for 6 hours.

Serving suggestion:

Serve over your favorite vegan pasta.

Tofu "Spaghetti" Quinoa

Hope Comerford
Clinton Township, MI

Makes 8–10 servings
Prep. Time: 5 minutes   ⚬   Cooking Time: 5 hours   ⚬   Ideal slow-cooker size: 5- or 6-qt.

32 oz. meatless crumbles

½ tsp. salt

⅛ tsp. pepper

1 tsp. garlic powder

1 tsp. onion powder

1 cup quinoa

1 cup chopped onion

1 cup shredded vegan mozzarella cheese

4 cups tomato sauce

2 cups water

1. Spray crock with nonstick spray.

2. Place all ingredients in crock and stir.

3. Cover and cook on Low for 5 hours.

Baked Ziti

Hope Comerford
Clinton Township, MI

Makes 8 servings
Prep. Time: 15 minutes ⚶ *Cooking Time: 4 hours* ⚶ *Ideal slow-cooker size: 5-qt.*

28-oz. can low-sodium crushed tomatoes

15-oz. can low-sodium tomato sauce

1½ tsp. Italian seasoning

1 tsp. garlic powder

1 tsp. onion powder

1 tsp. pepper

1 tsp. sea salt

1 lb. ziti or rigatoni pasta, uncooked, divided

1–2 cups vegan shredded mozzarella cheese, divided

1. Spray crock with nonstick spray.

2. In a bowl, mix together crushed tomatoes, tomato sauce, Italian seasoning, garlic powder, onion powder, pepper, and salt.

3. In the bottom of the crock, pour ⅓ of the pasta sauce.

4. Add ½ of the pasta on top of the sauce.

5. Add another ⅓ of your pasta sauce.

6. Spread ½ of the vegan mozzarella cheese on top of that.

7. Add the remaining pasta, the remaining sauce, and the remaining vegan cheese on top of that.

8. Cover and cook on Low for 4 hours.

Faked You Out Alfredo

Sue Hamilton
Benson, AZ

Makes 4 servings
Prep. Time: 5 minutes & Cooking Time: 6 hours & Ideal slow-cooker size: 3-qt.

1-lb. bag of frozen cauliflower
13½-oz. can light coconut milk
½ cup diced onion
2 cloves garlic, minced
1 Tbsp. vegetable stock concentrate
salt and pepper, to taste

1. Place the frozen cauliflower, coconut milk, onion, garlic, and the vegetable stock concentrate in your crock. Stir mixture to blend in the stock concentrate.

2. Cover and cook on Low for 6 hours.

3. Place cooked mixture in blender and process until smooth.

4. Add salt and pepper to taste.

Serving suggestion:

Serve over regular pasta or veggie pasta or cooked sliced potatoes.

TIP

• This is great with mushrooms mixed in.

• This sauce can be made ahead of time and refrigerated.

Mexi Rotini

Jane Geigley
Lancaster, PA

Makes 6 servings
Prep. Time: 30 minutes & Cooking Time: 4½ hours & Ideal slow-cooker size: 4-qt.

I cup water

3 cups partially cooked rotini

12-oz. pkg. frozen mixed vegetables

10-oz. can Ro*Tel diced tomatoes with green chilies

4-oz. can green chilies, undrained

16 oz. meatless crumbles

I cup vegan shredded cheddar cheese

1. Combine all ingredients in slow cooker except vegan shredded cheddar.

2. Cover and cook on Low for 4 hours.

3. Top with the vegan shredded cheddar, then let cook covered an additional 20 minutes or so.

Side Dishes

Cauliflower Cassoulet

Susie Shenk Wenger
Lancaster, PA

Makes 6 servings
Prep. Time: 30 minutes ⚜ *Cooking Time: 4–6 hours* ⚜ *Ideal slow-cooker size: 6-qt.*

1 cup uncooked brown rice

½ tsp. kosher salt

2 cups water

1 cup sliced fresh mushrooms

1 large sweet onion, chopped

½ cup chopped red bell pepper

3 cloves garlic, chopped

1 Tbsp. vegan butter

1 Tbsp. olive oil

1 large head cauliflower, chopped

½ cup diced nutritional yeast

1 tsp. dried basil

½ tsp. dried oregano

salt and pepper, to taste

juice and zest of 1 lemon

1. Put rice and ½ tsp. salt in lightly greased slow cooker. Pour water over rice.

2. Sprinkle in mushrooms, onion, bell pepper, and garlic. Sprinkle lightly with salt and pepper. Dot with vegan butter and drizzle with olive oil.

3. Sprinkle in cauliflower and nutritional yeast. Sprinkle with basil and oregano, adding salt and pepper to taste.

4. Cover and cook on Low for 4–6 hours, until rice is cooked and cauliflower is tender.

5. Drizzle with lemon juice and zest before serving.

Broccoli and Bell Peppers

Frieda Weisz
Aberdeen, SD

Makes 8 servings
Prep. Time: 20 minutes ♣ Cooking Time: 4–5 hours ♣ Ideal slow-cooker size: 3½- or 4-qt.

2 lb. fresh broccoli, trimmed and chopped into bite-sized pieces

1 clove garlic, minced

1 green or red bell pepper, cut into thin slices

1 medium onion, peeled and cut into slices

¼ cup liquid aminos

½ tsp. salt

dash of black pepper

1 Tbsp. sesame seeds, optional, as garnish

1. Combine all ingredients except sesame seeds in slow cooker.

2. Cook on Low for 4–5 hours. Top with sesame seeds.

Lemony Garlic Asparagus

Hope Comerford
Clinton Township, MI

Makes 4 servings
Prep. Time: 5 minutes ♨ Cooking Time: 1½–2 hours ♨ Ideal slow-cooker size: 2- or 3-qt.

1 lb. asparagus, bottom inch (tough part) removed

1 Tbsp. olive oil

1½ Tbsp. lemon juice

3–4 cloves garlic, peeled and minced

¼ tsp. salt

⅛ tsp. pepper

1. Spray crock with vegan nonstick spray.

2. Lay asparagus at bottom of crock and coat with the olive oil.

3. Pour the lemon juice over the top, then sprinkle with the garlic, salt, and pepper.

4. Cover and cook on Low for 1½–2 hours.

Serving suggestion:

Garnish with diced pimento, garlic, and lemon zest.

Barbecued Green Beans

Janette Fox
Honey Brook, PA

Makes 4–6 servings
Prep. Time: 20 minutes ⚬ *Cooking Time: 3 hours* ⚬ *Ideal slow-cooker size: 3½-qt.*

1 qt. green beans, trimmed
1 cup water
¾ cup ketchup
⅓ cup brown sugar
1½ tsp. prepared mustard

1. Cook green beans with water, covered, until green beans are crisp-tender. Drain, but save the liquid.

2. Mix ketchup, brown sugar, mustard, cooked green beans and ½ cup bean liquid in slow cooker.

3. Cover. Cook on Low for 3 hours.

Fast and Fabulous Brussels Sprouts

Phyllis Good
Lancaster, PA

Makes 4–6 servings
Prep. Time: 15 minutes ❧ Cooking Time: 2–5 hours ❧ Ideal slow-cooker size: 2- or 3-qt.

1 lb. Brussels sprouts, bottoms trimmed off and halved

3 Tbsp. vegan butter, melted

1 ½ Tbsp. Dijon mustard

¼ tsp. salt

¼ tsp. freshly ground black pepper

¼ cup water

½ tsp. dried tarragon, optional

1. Mix all ingredients in slow cooker.

2. Cover and cook on High for 2–2½ hours, or Low for 4–5 hours, until sprouts are just soft. Some of the Brussels sprouts at the sides will get brown and crispy, and this is delicious.

3. Stir well to distribute sauce. Serve hot or warm.

Zucchini Casserole

Hope Comerford
Clinton Township, MI

Makes 4–6 servings
Prep. Time: 15 minutes ⚜ Cooking Time: 3 hours ⚜ Ideal slow-cooker size: 3-qt.

4 medium zucchini, sliced

I large yellow onion, sliced in half rings

I red pepper, sliced

14½-oz. can diced tomatoes

I tsp. sea salt

I tsp. Italian seasoning

2 Tbsp. vegan butter

¼ cup vegan shredded Parmesan cheese

1. Spray crock with nonstick spray.

2. In the crock, mix the zucchini, onion, red pepper, diced tomatoes, sea salt, and Italian seasoning.

3. Spread the vegan butter evenly across the contents of the crock.

4. Sprinkle the vegan Parmesan cheese on top.

5. Cover and cook on Low for 3 hours.

Slow-Cooker Beets

Hope Comerford
Clinton Township, MI

Makes 4–6 servings
Prep. Time: 10 minutes ❧ *Cooking Time: 3–4 hours* ❧ *Ideal slow-cooker size: 3-qt.*

4–6 large beets, scrubbed well and tops removed

3 Tbsp. olive oil

I tsp. sea salt

¼ tsp. pepper

3 Tbsp. balsamic vinegar

I Tbsp. lemon juice

1. Use foil to make a packet around each beet.

2. Divide the olive oil, salt, pepper, balsamic vinegar, and lemon juice evenly between each packet.

3. Place each beet packet into the slow cooker.

4. Cover and cook on Low for 3–4 hours, or until the beets are tender when poked with a knife.

5. Remove each beet packet from the crock and allow to cool and let the steam escape. Once cool enough to handle, use a paring knife to gently peel the skin off each beet. Cut into bite-sized pieces and serve with juice from the packet over the top.

Brown Sugar Glazed Carrots

Michele Ruvola
Vestal, NY

Makes 10 servings
Prep. Time: 5 minutes ⚶ Cooking Time: 4 minutes ⚶ Setting: Steam
Pressure: High ⚶ Release: Manual

32-oz. bag of baby carrots
½ cup vegetable broth
½ cup brown sugar
4 Tbsp. vegan butter
½ Tbsp. salt

1. Place all ingredients in inner pot of the Instant Pot.

2. Secure the lid, turn valve to sealing, and set timer for 4 minutes on Manual at high pressure.

3. When cooking time is up, perform a quick release to release pressure.

4. Stir carrots, then serve.

Mushrooms in Red Wine

Donna Lantgen
Arvada, CO

Makes 4 servings
Prep. Time: 5 minutes ⚜ *Cooking Time: 4–6 hours* ⚜ *Ideal slow-cooker size: 3-qt.*

1 lb. whole fresh mushrooms, cleaned
4 cloves garlic, minced
¼ cup chopped onions
1 Tbsp. olive oil
1 cup vegan red wine
½ tsp. salt
⅛ tsp. pepper
¼ tsp. dried thyme

1. Mix ingredients in slow cooker.

2. Cover. Cook on Low 4–6 hours.

Potatoes with Parsley

Colleen Heatwole
Burton, MI

Makes 4 servings
Prep. Time: 10 minutes ⚕ Cooking Time: 5 minutes ⚕ Setting: Sauté then Manual
Pressure: High ⚕ Release: Manual

3 Tbsp. vegan butter, divided

2 lb. medium red potatoes (about 2 oz. each), halved lengthwise

1 clove garlic, minced

½ tsp. salt

½ cup vegetable broth

2 Tbsp. chopped fresh parsley

1. Place 1 Tbsp. vegan butter in the inner pot of the Instant Pot and select Sauté.

2. After vegan butter is melted, add potatoes, garlic, and salt, stirring well.

3. Sauté 4 minutes, stirring frequently.

4. Add vegetable broth and stir well.

5. Seal lid, make sure vent is on sealing, then select Manual for 5 minutes on high pressure.

6. When cooking time is up, manually release the pressure.

7. Strain potatoes, toss with remaining 2 Tbsp. vegan butter and chopped parsley, and serve immediately.

Wild Italian Mushrooms

Connie Johnson
Loudon, NH

Makes 4–5 servings
Prep. Time: 20 minutes ⚜ *Cooking Time: 6–8 hours* ⚜ *Ideal slow-cooker size: 5-qt.*

2 large onions, chopped

3 large red bell peppers, chopped

3 large green bell peppers, chopped

2–3 Tbsp. olive oil

12-oz. pkg. oyster mushrooms, cleaned and chopped

4 cloves garlic, minced

3 fresh bay leaves

10 fresh basil leaves, chopped

1 tsp. salt

1½ tsp. pepper

28-oz. can Italian plum tomatoes, crushed, or chopped

1. Sauté onions and peppers in oil in skillet until soft. Stir in mushrooms and garlic. Sauté just until mushrooms begin to turn brown. Pour into slow cooker.

2. Add remaining ingredients. Stir well.

3. Cover. Cook on Low 6–8 hours. Remove bay leaves and serve.

Corn on the Cob

Donna Conto
Saylorsburg, PA

Makes 3–4 servings
Prep. Time: 10 minutes & *Cooking Time: 2–3 hours* & *Ideal slow-cooker size: 5- or 6-qt.*

6–8 ears of corn (in husk)
½ cup water

1. Remove silk from corn, as much as possible, but leave husks on.

2. Cut off ends of corn so ears can stand in the cooker.

3. Add water.

4. Cover. Cook on Low 2–3 hours.

 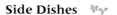

Spicy Roasted Butternut Squash

Marilyn Mowry
Irving, TX

Makes 15–20 servings
Prep. Time: 1 hour ❧ Cooking Time: 4–6 hours ❧ Ideal slow-cooker size: 6-qt.

¼ cup olive oil

2 tsp. ground cinnamon, divided

½ tsp. ground cumin

1¾ tsp. salt, divided

5-lb. butternut squash, split in quarters and seeds removed

2 carrots, diced

1 large white onion, diced

2 Granny Smith apples, peeled, cored, and quartered

4 chipotles in adobo sauce, seeds scraped out, chopped

roughly 10 cups vegetable stock

1. Mix olive oil, 1 tsp. cinnamon, ground cumin, and ¾ tsp. salt in mixing bowl. Brush over the flesh of the quartered squash.

2. Place squash cut side down on a rimmed baking sheet lined with foil.

3. Add carrots, onion, and apples to bowl with oil and toss. Spread on another foil-lined sheet.

4. Roast both trays 40–50 minutes at 425°F until squash is soft and onion mix is golden brown. Scoop out the squash.

5. Put squash, veggie mix, chipotles, 1 tsp. salt, and 1 tsp. cinnamon in slow cooker. Add vegetable stock.

6. Cover and cook on High 4 hours or Low for 6 hours. Mash with a potato masher or puree with immersion blender.

"Baked" Sweet Potatoes

Hope Comerford
Clinton Township, MI

Makes 5 potatoes
Prep. Time: 2 minutes ⚬ *Cooking Time: 4–5 hours* ⚬ *Ideal slow-cooker size: 5- or 6-qt.*

5 sweet potatoes, pierced in several places with a fork or knife

1. Place sweet potatoes in slow cooker.

2. Cover and cook on Low for 4–5 hours, or until they are tender when poked with a fork or knife.

Thyme Roasted Sweet Potatoes

Hope Comerford
Clinton Township, MI

Makes 6 servings
Prep. Time: 20 minutes ❧ *Cooking Time: 7 hours* ❧ *Ideal slow-cooker size: 4-qt.*

4–6 medium sweet potatoes, peeled, cubed

3 Tbsp. olive oil

5–6 large cloves garlic, minced

⅓ cup fresh thyme leaves

½ tsp. kosher salt

¼ tsp. red pepper flakes

1. Place all ingredients into the crock and stir.

2. Cover and cook on Low for 7 hours, or until potatoes are tender.

Sweet Potato Puree

Colleen Heatwole
Burton, MI

Makes 4–6 servings
Prep. Time: 10 minutes ⚶ *Cooking Time: 6 minutes* ⚶ *Setting: Manual*
Pressure: High ⚶ *Release: Manual*

3 lb. sweet potatoes, peeled and cut
into roughly 2-inch cubes

1 cup water

2 Tbsp. vegan butter

1 tsp. salt

2 tsp. packed brown sugar

2 tsp. lemon juice

½ tsp. cinnamon

⅛ tsp. nutmeg, optional

1. Place sweet potatoes and water in inner pot of the Instant Pot.

2. Secure the lid, make sure vent is at sealing, then cook for 6 minutes on high using the Manual setting.

3. Manually release the pressure when cook time is up.

4. Drain sweet potatoes and place in large mixing bowl. Mash with potato masher or hand mixer.

5. Once thoroughly mashed, add remaining ingredients.

6. Taste and adjust seasonings to taste.

7. Serve immediately while still hot.

German Potato Salad

Hope Comerford
Clinton Township, MI

Makes 6 servings
Prep. Time: 20 minutes ⚬ *Cooking Time: 5 hours* ⚬ *Ideal slow-cooker size: 4-qt.*

1½ lb. red potatoes, coarsely chopped

1 medium onion, chopped

2 slices vegan bacon strips, chopped

1 cup chopped celery

¼ cup apple cider vinegar

2 Tbsp. whole-grain mustard

1 Tbsp. olive oil

½ tsp. sea salt

¼ tsp. pepper

1 Tbsp. cornstarch

1. Place potatoes, onion, vegan bacon, and celery in crock.

2. In a small bowl, combine the apple cider vinegar, mustard, olive oil, salt, pepper, and cornstarch. Pour this over the contents of the crock and stir.

3. Cover and cook on Low for 5 hours or until potatoes are tender.

Quinoa with Vegetables

Hope Comerford
Clinton Township, MI

Makes 4–6 servings
Prep. Time: 10 minutes ❧ *Cooking Time: 4–6 hours* ❧ *Ideal slow-cooker size: 3-qt.*

2 cups quinoa

4 cups vegetable stock

½ cup chopped onion

1 Tbsp. olive oil

1 medium red pepper, chopped

1 medium yellow pepper, chopped

1 medium carrot, chopped

3 cloves garlic, minced

½ tsp. sea salt

¼ tsp. pepper

1 Tbsp. fresh cilantro, chopped

1. Place quinoa, vegetable stock, onion, olive oil, red pepper, yellow pepper, carrot, garlic, salt, and pepper into crock and stir.

2. Cook on Low for 4–6 hours or until liquid is absorbed and quinoa is tender.

3. Top with fresh cilantro to serve.

Savory Rice

Jane Geigley
Lancaster, PA

Makes 6–8 servings
Prep. Time: 10 minutes ❧ *Cooking Time: 3–4 hours* ❧ *Ideal slow-cooker size: 4-qt.*

2 cups uncooked short-grain
brown rice

5 cups water

1 Tbsp. coconut oil

½ tsp. ground thyme

2 Tbsp. dried parsley

2 tsp. garlic powder

1 tsp. dried basil

1. Mix rice, water, coconut oil, thyme, parsley, garlic powder, basil, and salt.

2. Pour into slow cooker. Cover.

3. Cook on High for 3–4 hours or until water is absorbed.

Rice Guiso

Cynthia Hockman-Chupp
Canby, OR

Makes 3–6 servings
Prep. Time: 5 minutes ⚘ Cooking Time: 15 minutes ⚘ Setting: Rice
Pressure: High ⚘ Release: Natural or Manual

I Tbsp. coconut oil

I medium onion, chopped

I cup rice

I tsp. salt

⅛ tsp. pepper

¼–½ cup chopped bell pepper, any color (or a variety of colors!)

I–I⅛ cups water

2 Tbsp. tomato paste

1. Place all ingredients in inner pot of the Instant Pot. Stir.

2. Secure the lid and make sure vent is at sealing. Push rice button and set for 15 minutes. Allow to cook.

3. Use manual release for a final product that is more moist, natural release for a slightly drier rice. I prefer natural release for this rice.

Beans & Rice

Kris Zimmerman
Lititz, PA

Makes 6–8 servings
Prep. Time: 15 minutes ⚜ *Cooking Time: 3–4 hours* ⚜ *Ideal slow-cooker size: 3-qt.*

3 cups cooked beans of your choice, rinsed and drained

1 cup brown rice

14½-oz. can diced tomatoes

1 Tbsp. coconut oil, melted

salt, to taste

1 tsp. cumin

½ tsp. garlic powder

2 cups water

diced green chilies, optional

hot sauce or cayenne pepper, optional

1. Place all ingredients in slow cooker and stir well.

2. Cover and cook on High for 3–4 hours. Begin checking at 3–3½ hours to see if your rice is done.

Desserts

Creamy Rice Pudding

Colleen Heatwole
Burton, MI

Makes 10 servings
Prep. Time: 5 minutes   ❧   Cooking Time: 15 minutes   ❧   Setting: Sauté then Manual
Pressure: Low   ❧   Release: Manual

1½ cups arborio rice

2 cups non-dairy milk

14-oz. can coconut milk, light preferred

1 cup water

½ cup granulated sugar

2 tsp. cinnamon

½ tsp. salt

1½ tsp. vanilla extract

1 cup dried tart cherries or golden raisins

1. Rinse rice and drain.

2. Place rice, non-dairy milk, coconut milk, water, sugar, cinnamon, and salt in the inner pot of the Instant Pot.

3. Select Sauté and bring to boil, stirring constantly to dissolve sugar.

4. As soon as mixture comes to a boil, turn off Sauté.

5. Secure lid and make sure vent is at sealing. Using Manual mode, select 15 minutes and low pressure.

6. When cook time is up, manually release the pressure.

7. Remove lid and add vanilla and dried fruit. Stir.

8. Place cover on pot but do not turn on.

9. Let stand for 15 minutes, then stir and serve.

Coconut Rice Pudding

Hope Comerford
Clinton Township, MI

Makes 6 servings
Prep. Time: 5 minutes ⚶ *Cooking Time: 2½ hours* ⚶ *Ideal slow-cooker size: 5- or 6-qt.*

2½ cups coconut milk
14-oz. can light coconut milk
½ cup turbinado sugar
1 cup arborio rice
1 stick cinnamon
1 cup dried cranberries, optional

1. Spray crock with nonstick spray.

2. In crock, whisk together the coconut milk, canned coconut milk, and sugar.

3. Add in the rice and cinnamon stick.

4. Cover and cook on Low about 2–2½ hours, or until rice is tender and the pudding has thickened.

5. Remove cinnamon stick. If using cranberries, sprinkle on top of each bowl of Coconut Rice Pudding.

Baked Apples

Judy Gascho
Woodburn, OR

Makes 6 servings
Prep. Time: 15 minutes & Cooking Time: 9 minutes & Setting: Manual
Pressure: High & Release: Natural then Manual

6 medium apples, cored
1 cup apple juice or cider
¼ cup raisins or dried cranberries
½ cup brown sugar
1 tsp. cinnamon

1. Put the apples into the inner pot of the Instant Pot.

2. Pour in the apple juice or cider. Sprinkle the raisins, sugar, and cinnamon over the apples.

3. Close and lock the lid and be sure the steam vent is in the sealing position.

4. Cook for 9 minutes on Manual mode at high pressure.

5. When time is up, unplug and turn off the pressure cooker. Let pressure release naturally for 15 minutes, then manually release any remaining pressure.

6. Take off lid and remove apples to individual small bowls, adding cooking liquid to each.

Apple Cake

Sue Hamilton
Minooka, IL

Makes 8 servings
Prep. Time: 20 minutes ❧ Cooking Time: 2½–3 hours ❧ Ideal slow-cooker size: 4-qt.

1½ Tbsp. ground flaxseed
4½ Tbsp. water
1 cup flour
¾ cup sugar
2 tsp. baking powder
1 tsp. ground cinnamon
¼ tsp. salt
4 medium-sized cooking apples, chopped
2 tsp. vanilla extract

1. Mix together the flaxseed and water in a bowl and set aside to thicken approximately 3 minutes.

2. Combine flour, sugar, baking powder, cinnamon, and salt.

3. Add apples, stirring lightly to coat.

4. Combine thickened flaxseed/water mixture and vanilla. Add to apple mixture. Stir until just moistened. Spoon into lightly greased slow cooker.

5. Cover. Bake on High 2½–3 hours.

6. Serve warm.

Healthy Coconut Apple Crisp

Hope Comerford
Clinton Township, MI

Makes 8–9 servings
Prep. Time: 20 minutes ☙ Cooking Time: 2 hours ☙ Ideal slow-cooker size: 3- or 4-qt.

5 medium Granny Smith apples, peeled, cored, sliced
1 Tbsp. cinnamon
¼ tsp. nutmeg
1 tsp. vanilla

Crumble:
1 cup gluten-free oats
½ cup coconut flour
½ cup unsweetened coconut flakes
1 tsp. cinnamon
⅛ tsp. nutmeg
½ tsp. sea salt
2 Tbsp. vegan "honey"
2 Tbsp. coconut oil, melted
2–3 Tbsp. unsweetened coconut milk

1. Spray crock with vegan nonstick spray.

2. In the crock, combine apple slices, cinnamon, nutmeg, and vanilla.

3. In a medium bowl, combine all of the crumble ingredients. If too dry, add a bit more vegan "honey" or coconut milk. Pour over top of apple mixture.

4. Cover and cook on Low for 2 hours.

Serving suggestion:

Serve with vegan vanilla ice cream.

Strawberry Mint Crisp

Hope Comerford
Clinton Township, MI

Makes 4 servings
Prep. Time: 20 minutes & *Cooking Time: 2 hours* & *Ideal slow-cooker size: 2- or 3-qt.*

2½–3 cups sliced strawberries
1 tsp. cinnamon
½ tsp. mint extract
1 tsp. vanilla extract
3 Tbsp. fresh chopped mint

Crumble:
½ cup gluten-free oats
¼ cup gluten-free oat flour
½ tsp. cinnamon
¼ tsp. salt
1 Tbsp. vegan "honey"
1 Tbsp. coconut oil, melted
1–2 Tbsp. unsweetened almond or coconut milk

1. Spray crock with vegan nonstick spray.

2. In the crock, combine strawberries, cinnamon, mint extract, vanilla extract, and fresh chopped mint.

3. In a bowl, combine all the crumble ingredients. If it's too dry, add a bit more "honey" or milk of your choice. Pour this mixture into the crock.

4. Cover and cook on Low for 2 hours.

Serving suggestion:

Serve with vegan vanilla ice cream.

Nectarine Almond Crisp

Hope Comerford
Clinton Township, MI

Makes 8–9 servings
Prep. Time: 10 minutes ⚜ Cooking Time: 2 hours ⚜ Ideal slow-cooker size: 3- or 4-qt.

5 nectarines, cored and sliced

¼ cup slivered almonds

1 tsp. cinnamon

¼ tsp. nutmeg

¼ tsp. ginger

1 tsp. vanilla extract

Crumble:

1 cup gluten-free oats

½ cup almond flour

½ cup slivered almonds

1 tsp. cinnamon

¼ tsp. ginger

½ tsp. sea salt

2 Tbsp. vegan "honey"

2 Tbsp. coconut oil, melted

2–3 Tbsp. unsweetened almond milk

1. Spray crock with vegan nonstick spray.

2. In the crock, combine nectarines, almonds, cinnamon, nutmeg, ginger, and vanilla.

3. In a medium bowl, combine all the crumble ingredients. If the mixture is too dry, add a bit more "honey" or almond milk. Pour over the top of the nectarine mixture.

4. Cover and cook on Low for 2 hours.

Serving suggestion:

Serve with vegan vanilla ice cream.

Blueberry Crinkle

Phyllis Good
Lancaster, PA

Makes 6–8 servings
Prep. Time: 15–20 minutes & Cooking Time: 2–3 hours & Ideal slow-cooker size: 3- or 4-qt.

⅓ cup turbinado sugar
¾ cup gluten-free oats
½ cup gluten-free flour
½ tsp. cinnamon
dash of kosher salt
6 Tbsp. coconut oil, cold
4 cups blueberries, fresh or frozen
2 Tbsp. maple syrup
2 Tbsp. instant tapioca
2 Tbsp. lemon juice
½ tsp. lemon zest

1. Grease interior of slow-cooker crock.

2. In a large bowl, combine turbinado sugar, oats, gluten-free flour, cinnamon, and salt.

3. Using two knives, a pastry cutter, or your fingers, work coconut oil into dry ingredients until small crumbs form.

4. In a separate bowl, stir together blueberries, maple syrup, tapioca, lemon juice, and lemon zest.

5. Spoon blueberry mixture into slow-cooker crock.

6. Sprinkle crumbs over blueberries.

7. Cover. Cook 2–3 hours on Low, or until firm in the middle with juice bubbling up around the edges.

8. Remove lid with a giant swoop away from yourself so condensation on inside of lid doesn't drip on the crumbs.

9. Lift crock out of cooker. Let cool until either warm or room temperature before eating.

Quick Yummy Peaches

Willard E. Roth
Elkhart, IN

Makes 6 servings
Prep. Time: 5–20 minutes ⚭ *Cooking Time: 5 hours* ⚭ *Ideal slow-cooker size: 3-qt.*

⅓ cup vegan baking mix
⅔ cup gluten-free oats
⅓ cup maple syrup
1 tsp. ground cinnamon
4 cups sliced fresh peaches
½ cup water

1. Mix together baking mix, oats, maple syrup, and cinnamon in greased slow cooker.

2. Stir in peaches and water.

3. Cook on Low for at least 5 hours. (If you like a drier cobbler, remove lid for last 15–30 minutes of cooking.)

Homestyle Bread Pudding

Lizzie Weaver
Ephrata, PA

Makes 6 servings
Prep. Time: 10–15 minutes ⚜ Cooking Time: 2–3 hours
Ideal slow-cooker size: large enough to hold your baking insert

1½ Tbsp. ground flaxseed
4½ Tbsp. water
2¼ cups non-dairy milk
½ tsp. ground cinnamon
¼ tsp. salt
⅓ cup maple syrup
1 tsp. vanilla extract
2 cups 1-inch vegan bread cubes
½ cup raisins

1. Mix together the flaxseed and water in a bowl and set aside for approximately 3 minutes, to thicken.

2. Once flaxseed/water mixture has thickened, combine all ingredients in bowl. Pour into slow-cooker baking insert. Cover baking insert. Place on metal rack (or rubber jar rings) in bottom of slow cooker.

3. Pour ½ cup hot water into cooker around outside of insert.

4. Cover slow cooker. Cook on High 2–3 hours.

5. Serve pudding warm or cold.

Upside-Down Apple "Pie"

Hope Comerford
Clinton Township, MI

Makes 6 servings
Prep. Time: 15 minutes ✤ *Cooking Time: 6 hours* ✤ *Ideal slow-cooker size: 6-qt.*

2 Tbsp. ground flaxseed

6 Tbsp. water

8 Gala apples, peeled, cored, and sliced

1½ tsp. apple pie spice

¾ cup non-dairy milk

½ cup turbinado sugar

1½ cups Bisquick, divided

5 Tbsp. coconut oil, divided

1½ tsp. vanilla extract

¼ cup brown sugar

1. Mix together the flaxseed and water and set aside until thickened, approximately 3 minutes.

2. Line the crock with parchment paper and spray with vegan nonstick spray.

3. Place the apples and apple pie spice into the crock and stir.

4. In a medium-sized bowl, mix together the non-dairy milk, turbinado sugar, flaxseed/water mixture, ½ cup Bisquick, 2 Tbsp. of melted coconut oil, and the vanilla. Pour this over the apples.

5. In a small bowl, mix together the remaining Bisquick, coconut oil, and the brown sugar. It will be crumbly. Sprinkle this evenly over the contents of the crock.

6. Secure the lid of the slow cooker with some paper towels under it to absorb moisture.

7. Cook on Low for 6 hours.

Pineapple Bread Pudding

Janie Canupp
Millersville, MD

Makes 10 servings
Prep. Time: 15 minutes ⚬ *Cooking Time: 2–3 hours* ⚬ *Ideal slow-cooker size: 4-qt.*

3 Tbsp. ground flaxseed

½ cup water plus 1 Tbsp. water

2 Tbsp. flour

⅓ cup sugar

2 (8-oz.) cans chunky pineapple, with juice

6 slices vegan bread

5⅓ Tbsp. (⅓ cup) vegan butter

1. Combine flaxseed and water in a bowl and let sit until thickened, approximately 3 minutes.

2. Mix flour, sugar and thickened flaxseed/water mixture until smooth. Stir in pineapple and juice. Set aside.

3. Break bread in small chunks and place in greased slow cooker.

4. Melt vegan butter and pour over bread.

5. Pour pineapple mixture over bread.

6. Cover and cook on Low for 2–3 hours, until brown and firm.

Dump Cake

Janie Steele
Moore, OK

Makes 8–10 servings
Prep. Time: 10 minutes ⚬ *Cooking Time: 12 minutes* ⚬ *Setting: Manual*
Pressure: High ⚬ *Release: Manual*

6 Tbsp. vegan butter

1 vegan box cake mix

2 (20-oz.) cans vegan pie filling

1. Mix vegan butter and dry cake mix in bowl. It will be clumpy.

2. Pour pie filling in the inner pot of the Instant Pot.

3. Pour the dry mix over top.

4. Secure lid and make sure vent is at sealing. Cook for 12 minutes on Manual mode at high pressure.

5. Release pressure manually when cook time is up and remove lid to prevent condensation from getting into cake.

6. Let stand 5–10 minutes.

Serving suggestion:

Serve with your favorite vegan ice cream.

Lotsa Chocolate Almond Cake

Hope Comerford
Clinton Township, MI

Makes 10 servings
Prep. Time: 10 minutes ⚜ *Cooking Time: 3 hours* ⚜ *Cooling Time: 30 minutes* ⚜ *Ideal slow-cooker size: 6-qt.*

4 Tbsp. ground flaxseed
¾ cup water
1 ½ cups almond flour
¾ cup turbinado sugar
⅔ cup cocoa powder
¼ cup vegan chocolate protein powder
2 tsp. baking powder
¼ tsp. salt
½ cup coconut oil, melted
¾ cup almond milk
1 tsp. vanilla extract
1 tsp. almond extract
¾ cup vegan dark chocolate chips

1. Mix together the flaxseed and water in a bowl and set aside to thicken, approximately 3 minutes.

2. Cover any hot spot of your crock with aluminum foil, and spray crock with vegan nonstick spray.

3. In a bowl, mix together the almond flour, sugar, cocoa powder, protein powder, baking powder, and salt.

4. In a different bowl, mix together the coconut oil, thickened flaxseed/water mixture, almond milk, and vanilla and almond extracts.

5. Pour wet ingredients into dry ingredients and mix until well combined. Stir in chocolate chips.

6. Pour cake mix into crock. Cover and cook on Low for 3 hours.

7. Turn the slow cooker off when the cooking time is over and let the cake cool in the crock for 30 minutes.

8. Place a plate or platter over the crock, then turn the crock upside down on the plate, so the cake releases onto the plate or platter.

Chocolate Peanut Butter Slow-Cooker Cake

Jennifer Freed
Harrisonburg, VA

Makes 12 servings
Prep. Time: 20 minutes ⚬ Cooking Time: 2–2½ hours ⚬ Ideal slow-cooker size: 4-qt.

I cup flour

I ¼ cups sugar, divided

¼ cup plus 3 Tbsp. cocoa powder, divided

I ½ tsp. baking powder

½ cup non-dairy milk

2 Tbsp. vegan butter, melted

I tsp. vanilla extract

2 cups boiling water

½ cup peanut butter

1. In a large mixing bowl, combine the flour, ½ cup sugar, 3 Tbsp. cocoa powder, and baking powder.

2. Whisk in the non-dairy milk, vegan butter, and vanilla, and mix until smooth.

3. Pour into a lightly greased slow cooker.

4. Combine the ¾ cup sugar and ¼ cup cocoa powder.

5. In a separate bowl, combine the boiling water and peanut butter and whisk till smooth.

6. Add to the cocoa and sugar mixture and mix until well combined. Pour over the batter in the slow cooker. Do not stir.

7. Cover. Cook on High for 2–2½ hours, until top is set and slightly puffy.

8. Use a spoon to dish from the slow cooker. Serve warm with ice cream.

Serving suggestion:

Serve with vegan ice cream.

Fudgy Secret Brownies

Juanita Weaver
Johnsonville, IL

Makes 8 servings
Prep. Time: 10 minutes ⚘ *Cooking Time: 1½–2 hours* ⚘ *Ideal slow-cooker size: 6- or 7-qt.*

4 oz. vegan unsweetened chocolate

¾ cup coconut oil

¾ cup frozen diced okra, partially thawed

6 oz. silken tofu

1½ cups xylitol or your choice of sweetener

1 teaspoon pure vanilla extract

¼ tsp. mineral salt

¾ cup coconut flour

½–¾ cup coarsely chopped walnuts or pecans, optional

1. Melt vegan unsweetened chocolate and coconut oil in small saucepan.

2. Put okra and silken tofu in blender. Blend until smooth.

3. Measure all other ingredients in mixing bowl.

4. Pour melted chocolate and okra over the dry ingredients and stir with fork just until mixed.

5. Pour into greased slow cooker.

6. Cover and cook on High for 1½–2 hours.

Serving suggestion:

Serve with vegan ice cream.

Black Bean Brownies

Juanita Weaver
Johnsonville, IL

Makes 6–8 servings
Prep. Time: 5 minutes & Cooking Time: 1½ hours & Ideal slow-cooker size: 5- or 6-qt.

15-oz. can of black beans, rinsed and drained

12 oz. silken tofu

⅓ cup cocoa powder

1½ tsp. aluminum-free baking powder

½ tsp. baking soda

2 Tbsp. coconut oil

2 tsp. pure vanilla extract

⅓ cup non-dairy Greek yogurt or vegan cottage cheese

¾ cup xylitol or your choice of sweetener

¼ tsp. salt

1. Put all ingredients in a food processor or blender. Blend until smooth.

2. Pour into greased slow cooker.

3. Cover and cook for 1½ hours on High.

4. Cool in crock. For best taste, chill before serving.

Zucchini Chocolate Chip Bars

Hope Comerford
Clinton Township, MI

Makes 8–10 servings
Prep. Time: 10 minutes 🦴 Cooking Time: 2–3 hours
Cooling Time: 30 minutes 🦴 Ideal slow-cooker size: 3-qt.

3 Tbsp. ground flaxseed

½ cup plus 1 Tbsp. water

¾ cup turbinado sugar

1 cup all-natural applesauce

3 tsp. vanilla extract

3 cups whole wheat flour

1 tsp. baking soda

½ tsp. baking powder

2 tsp. cinnamon

¼ tsp. salt

2 cups peeled and grated zucchini

1 cup vegan dark chocolate chips

1. Mix together the flaxseed and water in a bowl and set aside to thicken, approximately 3 minutes.

2. Spray the crock with vegan nonstick spray.

3. Mix together the thickened flaxseed/water mixture, sugar, applesauce, and vanilla.

4. In a separate bowl, mix together the flour, baking soda, baking powder, cinnamon, and salt. Add this to the wet mixture and stir just until everything is mixed well.

5. Stir in the zucchini and vegan chocolate chips.

6. Pour this mixture into the crock.

7. Cover and cook on Low for 2–3 hours. Let it cool in crock for about 30 minutes, then flip it over onto a serving platter or plate. It should come right out.

Metric Equivalent Measurements

If you're accustomed to using metric measurements, I don't want you to be inconvenienced by the imperial measurements I use in this book.

Use this handy chart, too, to figure out the size of the slow cooker you'll need for each recipe.

Weight (Dry Ingredients)

1 oz		30 g
4 oz	¼ lb	120 g
8 oz	½ lb	240 g
12 oz	¾ lb	360 g
16 oz	1 lb	480 g
32 oz	2 lb	960 g

Slow-Cooker Sizes

1-quart	0.96 l
2-quart	1.92 l
3-quart	2.88 l
4-quart	3.84 l
5-quart	4.80 l
6-quart	5.76 l
7-quart	6.72 l
8-quart	7.68 l

Volume (Liquid Ingredients)

½ tsp.		2 ml
1 tsp.		5 ml
1 Tbsp.	½ fl oz	15 ml
2 Tbsp.	1 fl oz	30 ml
¼ cup	2 fl oz	60 ml
⅓ cup	3 fl oz	80 ml
½ cup	4 fl oz	120 ml
⅔ cup	5 fl oz	160 ml
¾ cup	6 fl oz	180 ml
1 cup	8 fl oz	240 ml
1 pt	16 fl oz	480 ml
1 qt	32 fl oz	960 ml

Length

¼ in	6 mm
½ in	13 mm
¾ in	19 mm
1 in	25 mm
6 in	15 cm
12 in	30 cm

Recipe & Ingredient Index

About the Author

Hope Comerford is a mom, wife, elementary music teacher, blogger, recipe developer, public speaker, Young Living Essential Oils essential oil enthusiast/educator, and published author. In 2013, she was diagnosed with a severe gluten intolerance and since then has spent many hours creating easy, practical and delicious gluten-free recipes that can be enjoyed by both those who are affected by gluten and those who are not.

Growing up, Hope spent many hours in the kitchen with her Meme (grandmother) and her love for cooking grew from there. While working on her master's degree when her daughter was young, Hope turned to her slow cookers for some salvation and sanity. It was from there she began truly experimenting with recipes and quickly learned she had the ability to get a little more creative in the kitchen and develop her own recipes.

In 2010, Hope started her blog, *A Busy Mom's Slow Cooker Adventures*, to simply share the recipes she was making with her family and friends. She never imagined people all over the world would begin visiting her page and sharing her recipes with others as well. In 2013, Hope self-published her first cookbook, *Slow Cooker Recipes 10 Ingredients or Less and Gluten-Free*, and then later wrote *The Gluten-Free Slow Cooker*.

Hope became the new brand ambassador and author of Fix-It and Forget-It in mid-2016. Since then, she has brought her excitement and creativeness to the Fix-It and Forget-It brand. Through Fix-It and Forget-It, she has written *Fix-It and Forget-It Healthy Slow Cooker Cookbook, Forget-It Cooking for Two, Fix-It and Forget-It Instant Pot Cookbook, Fix-It and Forget-It Best 5-Ingredient Comfort Food Cookbook, Fix-it and Forget-It Plant-Based Keto Cookbook*, and many more.

Hope lives in the city of Clinton Township, Michigan, near Metro Detroit. She has been happily married to her husband and best friend, Justin, since 2008. Together they have two children, Ella and Gavin, who are her motivation, inspiration, and heart. In her spare time, Hope enjoys traveling, singing, cooking, reading books, spending time with friends and family, and relaxing.